WITHDRAWAL

# The High Renaissance

# GREAT ARTISTS OF THE WESTERN WORLD

# *The High Renaissance*

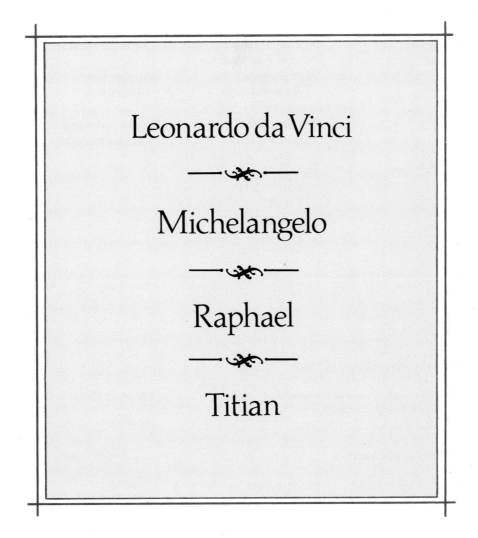

Leonardo da Vinci

Michelangelo

Raphael

Titian

MARSHALL CAVENDISH · LONDON · NEW YORK · SYDNEY

# Staff Credits

| | | | |
|---|---|---|---|
| **Editors** | Clive Gregory LL B<br>Sue Lyon BA (Honours) | **Picture Researchers** | Vanessa Fletcher BA<br>(Honours)<br>Flavia Howard BA<br>(Honours)<br>Jessica Johnson BA |
| **Art Editors** | Kate Sprawson BA<br>(Honours)<br>Keith Vollans LSIAD | **Production<br>Controllers** | Steve Roberts<br>Alan Stewart BSc |
| **Deputy Editor** | John Kirkwood B Sc<br>(Honours) | **Secretary** | Lynn Smail |
| **Sub-editors** | Caroline Bugler BA<br>(Honours), MA<br>Sue Churchill BA<br>(Honours)<br>Alison Cole BA, M Phil<br>Jenny Mohammadi<br>Nigel Rodgers BA<br>(Honours), MA<br>Penny Smith<br>Will Steeds BA<br>(Honours), MA | **Publisher**<br><br>**Editorial Director**<br><br>**Production<br>Executive**<br><br>**Consultant and<br>Authenticator** | Terry Waters Grad IOP<br><br>Maggi McCormick<br><br>Robert Paulley B Sc<br><br>Sharon Fermor BA<br>(Honours)<br>Lecturer in the<br>Extra-Mural<br>Department of<br>London University<br>and Lecturer in<br>Art History at<br>Sussex University |
| **Designers** | Stuart John<br>Julie Stanniland | | |

### Reference Edition 2001

Marshall Cavendish Corporation
99 White Plains Road
Tarrytown, NY 10591-9001

Printed in Malaysia

**Library of Congress Cataloging-in-Publication Data**

Great Artists of the Western World.

    Includes index.
    1. Artists—Biography.  I. Marshall Cavendish
Corporation
N40.G77 1987    709'.2'2 [B]    86—23863

ISBN 0-86307-743-9 (set)
    0-86307-745-5 (vol. 2)

# Preface

Looking at pictures can be one of the greatest pleasures that life has to offer. Note, however, those two words 'can be'; all too many of us remember all too clearly those grim afternoons of childhood when we were dragged, bored to tears and complaining bitterly, through room after room of Italian primitives by well-meaning relations or tight-lipped teachers. It was enough to put one off pictures for life – which, for some of us, was exactly what it did.

For if gallery-going is to be the fun it should be, certain conditions must be fulfilled. First, the pictures we are to see must be good pictures. Not necessarily great pictures – even a few of these can be daunting, while too many at a time may prove dangerously indigestible. But they must be well-painted, by good artists who know precisely both the effect they want to achieve and how best to achieve it. Second, we must limit ourselves as to quantity. Three rooms – four at the most – of the average gallery are more than enough for one day, and for best results we should always leave while we are still fresh, well before satiety sets in. Now I am well aware that this is a counsel of perfection: sometimes, in the case of a visiting exhibition or, perhaps, when we are in a foreign city with only a day to spare, we shall have no choice but to grit our teeth and stagger on to the end. But we shall not enjoy ourselves quite so much, nor will the pictures remain so long or so clearly in our memory.

The third condition is all-important: we must know something about the painters whose work we are looking at. And this is where this magnificent series of volumes – one of which you now hold in your hands – can make all the difference. No painting is an island: it must, if it is to be worth a moment's attention, express something of the personality of its painter. And that painter, however individual a genius, cannot but reflect the country, style and period, together with the views and attitudes of the people among whom he or she was born and bred. Even a superficial understanding of these things will illuminate a painting for us far better than any number of spotlights, and if in addition we have learnt something about the artist as a person – life and loves, character and beliefs, friends and patrons, and the places to which he or she travelled – the interest and pleasure that the work will give us will be multiplied a hundredfold.

Great Artists of the Western World will provide you with just such an insight into the life and work of some of the outstanding painters of Europe and America. The text is informative without ever becoming dry or academic, not limiting itself to the usual potted biographies but forever branching out into the contemporary world outside and beyond workshop or studio. The illustrations, in colour throughout, have been dispensed in almost reckless profusion. For those who, like me, revel in playing the Attribution Game – the object of which is to guess the painter of each picture before allowing one's eye to drop to the label – the little sections on 'Trademarks' are a particularly happy feature; but every aficionado will have particular preferences, and I doubt whether there is an art historian alive, however distinguished, who would not find some fascinating nugget of previously unknown information among the pages that follow.

This series, however, is not intended for art historians. It is designed for ordinary people like you and me – and for our older children – who are fully aware that the art galleries of the world constitute a virtually bottomless mine of potential enjoyment, and who are determined to extract as much benefit and advantage from it as they possibly can. All the volumes in this collection will enable us to do just that, expanding our knowledge not only of art itself but also of history, religion, mythology, philosophy, fashion, interior decoration, social customs and a thousand other subjects as well. So let us not simply leave them around, flipping idly through a few of their pages once in a while. Let us read them as they deserve to be read – and welcome a new dimension in our lives.

**John Julius Norwich** is a writer and broadcaster who has written histories of Venice and of Norman Sicily as well as several works on history, art and architecture. He has also made over twenty documentary films for television, including the recent **Treasure Houses of Britain** series which was widely acclaimed after repeated showings in the United States.

Lord Norwich is Chairman of the Venice in Peril Fund, and member of the Executive Committee of the British National Trust, an independently funded body established for the protection of places of historic interest and natural beauty.

# Contents

**Introduction** ———————————————————— 8
High Renaissance in Italy – painting in oil – sculpture as an art form –
symmetry and harmony – portrait painting in Venice

## Leonardo da Vinci ———————————————— 11

**The Artist's Life** ——————————————————— 12
Birth near Monte Albano – distrust of society – equestrian statue – drawings
– military engineer – death in France

**Gallery** —————————————————————————— 20
Religious works and portraits

**The Artist at Work** —————————————————— 30
Intellectual approach to art – mastering oil painting – sculpture and
architecture – making of a masterpiece

**In the Background: The Borgias** —————————— 36
A powerful family – Pope Alexander VI – Cesare Borgia

**A Year in the Life: 1492** ——————————————— 40
Death of Lorenzo de' Medici – Columbus – discovering the Americas

## Michelangelo ———————————————————— 43

**The Artist's Life** ——————————————————— 44
Early years in Florence – apprenticeship with Domenico Ghirlandaio – in
the Medici household – acclaim in Rome – the Sistine ceiling

**The Artist at Work** —————————————————— 50
The male nude – portraying emotions – fresco paintings – sculpture in
marble – the stonecarver's tools – architecture – making of a masterpiece

**Gallery** —————————————————————————— 54
Sculpture and the Sistine ceiling

**In the Background: New St Peter's** ———————— 68
Building a cathedral – financing the project – Michelangelo's
transformation – recreating the Latin cross – interior by Bernini

**A Year in the Life: 1527** ——————————————— 72
War between France and Italy – the storming of Rome – the new religion

## Raphael ——————————————————————— 75

**The Artist's Life** ——————————————————— 76
Boyhood familiarity with court – in the workshop of Pietro Perugino – the
young artist in Florence and Rome – appointment as Papal Architect –
marriage prospects – illness and early death

**The Artist at Work** —————————————— 82
Depicting the Virgin and Child – muscular nudes – influence of Leonardo
– animated faces and gestures – making of a masterpiece

**Gallery** —————————————— 86
Religious and historical paintings, and portraits

**In the Background: The Ruins of Ancient Rome** —————— 100
Rome in the 16th century – ruins of the old city – recapturing past glory –
finding building materials

**A Year in the Life: 1508** —————————— 104
The warrior-pope, Julius II – military alliance against Venice – defeat of the
city – Henry VIII of England

# Titian —————————————————— 107

**The Artist's Life** —————————————— 108
A Venetian apprenticeship – fresco painting with Giorgione – friends in
high places – Titian's last years

**The Artist at Work** —————————————— 114
Loose handling of forms and colours – using fingers and brushes – conveying
mood – workshop productions – making of a masterpiece

**Gallery** —————————————————— 120
Portraits, scenes from ancient mythology and religious works

**In the Background: The Holy Roman Emperor** —————— 132
Charles V – inheriting and running an empire – attack from all sides –
exhaustion and abdication

**A Year in the Life: 1572** —————————— 136
The Duke of Alva and the Sea Beggars – seizure of the port of Brill – the long
struggle begins – the Spanish Fury

# Appendix —————————————————— 139

**Gallery Guide** —————————————— 139
Where to see the works of Leonardo da Vinci, Michelangelo, Raphael and
Titian

**Bibliography** —————————————— 139

**Other High Renaissance Artists** —————————— 140
From the Bellini family to Jacopo Tintoretto – lives and major works of
artists of the High Renaissance

**Index** —————————————————— 142

# Introduction

Villa Farnesina, Rome

Leonardo da Vinci, Michelangelo, Raphael and Titian were the undisputed great masters of the 16th-century High Renaissance in Italy. Their highly individual works mark the culmination of three centuries of endeavour to revive the art of classical antiquity – and to improve upon it. A key development was the increased status of the artist: he was no longer a mere artisan, but came to be regarded as a super being, as intellectually creative as the philosophers.

## The Universal Man

Leonardo da Vinci was a man of powerful intellect whose constant experimentation took him far beyond the dry, hard manner of his contemporaries. It made him one of the great creators of the 16th-century High Renaissance – although born in 1452 and thus much older than Michelangelo (b.1475) or Raphael (b.1483). Unfortunately, however, his energies were spread over such a range of interests that hardly a single major enterprise was concluded. Thus, though he amassed thousands of notes and drawings, there was only a handful of paintings, few of which were completed. But what we have is work of genius.

His earliest datable work is an Arno landscape (p.13), drawn in 1473. This already shows his scientific interest in the structure of the earth and rock-formation. He also made meticulous studies of the way draperies fold and fall; whereas earlier and contemporary artists were perfectly content to represent drapery according to a set formula, Leonardo actually draped cloth and practised drawing realistic folds.

He also experimented with the new technique of oil painting, as in his Madonna in Munich; the realism of the crystal vase astonished his

Portraits below from left to right: Scala/Casa Buonarroti, Florence; Scala/Bibliotheque Royale, Turin; Scala/Uffizi, Florence; Gemäldegalerie Staatliche Museen Preussischer Kulturbesitz, Berlin (West)

Scala

## The Triumph of Galatea (1511)

(above) This shows Raphael's use of compositional symmetry – the same actions shown from different angles. The basic gestures of the nymph and sea-god in the left foreground are repeated by the couple on the right, and the swimming putto at the bottom of the scene echoes the movement of the figures at the top. This technique shows the interest of Renaissance artists in the human body.

contemporaries. He used oil again for the portrait of Ginevra de' Benci (p.22). The style of this half-length painting anticipates his Mona Lisa (p.28).

When commissioned by the monks of S Donato a Scopeta, near Florence, to paint the large Adoration of the Kings, 1481, Leonardo typically never finished the picture, but sufficient work was done to show his innovatory nature at work again. His composition sums up all the aims of late 15th-century Italian art: a pyramidal form that was dynamic yet compact. He also placed his Virgin at the centre of the group and holding their attention so that she is the dominant figure.

One of his few finished works – and the most famous – is his Mona Lisa (p.28), the mysterious portrait of the wife of a Florentine official. Painted c.1500/1504, it is important as developing a new type of portraiture, for its mastery of the new oil-technique and in particular for its sfumato effects – that is, blurred, softened outlines that lend an elusive quality to the features, suggesting inner depths and a personality that we cannot quite fathom. It is quite unlike the factual 'realistic' portraits of the period.

### The Divine Michelangelo

Michelangelo was in many ways the exact opposite of Leonardo da Vinci: reclusive rather than outgoing, and with no interest in science whatsoever. Yet he was similarly a man of many talents – sculptor, architect and even a composer of sonnets as well as being a painter.

On the death of his patron Lorenzo de' Medici and the rise to power of Savonarola in Florence (pp.45-6), Michelangelo went to Bologna and from

there in 1496, on to Rome. By the end of the century, he had carved his first major works: Bacchus (Bargello, Florence) and the Pietà (p.54).

In 1501, Michelangelo returned to Florence for four years during which he carved his David (p.55), another masterpiece and yet another original interpretation. He depicts David as the teenage youth of the biblical story, with gangling limbs and over-sized hands and feet just as they might be in nature. And in another sculpture of the period, the Bruges Madonna (Bruges, Notre-Dame), he breaks with the convention of seating the Christ Child on the Virgin's lap and instead places him at her knee, standing.

Michelangelo was also enormously influential in the development of Mannerism and indeed all subsequent Italian art, particularly after the completion of his greatest masterpiece: the ceiling of the Sistine Chapel (pp.56-67) which he painted entirely unaided. In this depiction of the creation of the world and the fall and punishment of man, he painted more than 300 figures, making much use of foreshortening and placing them in every conceivable pose.

### The Princely Painter

Raphael (1483-1520) was only 37 when he died – at the height of his fame – but in his short lifetime he equalled Leonardo and Michelangelo in stature and achievement. He was above all a master of symmetry and harmony.

Born the son of the painter Giovanni Santi, by

**High-renaissance artists**
(left to right) Jacopino del Conte's portrait of Michelangelo showing his crushed, misshapen nose which was broken during an argument. A self-portrait of Leonardo da Vinci – the versatile genius of the Renaissance – aged about 60. A self-portrait of the youthful Raphael. A self-portrait of Titian painted in about 1550 when he was in his 60s.

**Madonna della Sedia**
(below) One of Raphael's many depictions of the Virgin and Child which, despite his methodical approach to painting, shows an apparent naturalness and spontaneity. This idealized form of the mother was considered by the later artist Ingres (1780-1867) to be the embodiment of feminine grace and sweetness.

Santa Maria dei Frari, Venice

**The Pesaro Madonna (1519-26) by Titian**
(above) This painting was commissioned from Jacopo Pesaro, a Venetian nobleman, as a mark of thanksgiving for his victory over the Turks. On the left-hand side of the painting Jacopo kneels in front of the Virgin, while a standard-bearer brings forward a Turkish prisoner.

1500 he was working in the studio of Perugino and at about this time painted the Knight's Dream, now displayed in the National Gallery, London. It was this work that revealed him as a prodigy.

In 1504 Raphael left Perugino for Florence and his output of work there demonstrates how rapidly he assimilated all that the Florentine artists could teach him. Leonardo's experiments in chiaroscuro (the balance between light and shade) are echoed in the dark background of Raphael's Madonna del Granduca (p.84). And from the Mona Lisa he learned a new style of portraiture which he then adapted and used for his own Maddalena Doni

(Pitti, Florence). Michelangelo inspired a new power and severity in Raphael's drawing, as in the Deposition (Borghese, Rome).

Towards the end of 1508, Raphael went to Rome. His two most important frescoes there, the School of Athens (p.96) and Disputation on the Sacrament (p.98), are among the best examples of High Renaissance art: balanced and calm.

In Rome, Raphael received many commissions, which often meant that he was helped by his assistants; The Sistine Madonna (p.94) is unusual in that it was solely his own work. It is important because it shows how the simple, naturalistic image of the Madonna prevalent in the 15th century had changed in the 16th century to that of a superhuman being.

### Venice's Master Painter
Titian (c.1487/90-1576) was the only one of these four artists to remain for much of his life outside the influence of Florence and Rome. The greatest Venetian painter, he seems to have been a pupil first of Gentile Bellini and then of his brother, Giovanni.

After Giorgione's death in 1510, and the departure to Rome of his other nearest rival, Sebastiano del Pembo, Titian quickly established himself as the favourite portrait painter of the leading families in Venice, and in the process developed his own highly individual style. His subjects were painted in animated poses designed to bring out some special characteristic.

By 1532, Titian was in Bologna, where he met the Emperor Charles V and began a working relationship that was to develop into friendship. While visiting the Imperial court at Augsburg, Titian painted his greatest portrait: the equestrian study of Charles V on Horseback (p.129).

After Charles V's abdication, in 1555, Titian worked for his successor, Philip II, and produced an important series of religious works and some brilliant, rather erotic mythological paintings (p.131). He also developed a distinctively free handling of paint, spreading thick pigment with broad strokes of the brush, or with his fingers.

In his Christ Crowned with Thorns, (c.1565 Bavarian State Collections, Munich) this style is carried to its limits with no solid, light-reflecting surfaces. This was a radical departure from the careful preparatory work of his contemporaries, who still sketched out their ideas before transferring them to the canvas and colouring them in.

# Leonardo Da Vinci
## 1452-1519

Leonardo da Vinci was not only one of the greatest artists of the Renaissance, but also perhaps the most versatile genius who ever lived. His interests embraced virtually every field of study then known; anatomy and geology were two of his passions, and his great dream was man-powered flight. However, his perfectionism meant that he finished comparatively few major paintings.

Leonardo was born near Florence, but the scene of his most ambitious artistic undertakings was Milan. He spent his last years in France as the guest of King Francis I, revered as no previous artist had been. Although so many of his projects were unfulfilled, his marvellous drawings are eloquent testimony to the power of his incomparably inventive mind.

# The Universal Man

**Leonardo characterizes the spirit of the Renaissance: he spent his life in the pursuit of knowledge, and was as revered for his vast intellect as he was for his astonishing skill as an artist.**

Leonardo da Vinci was born on 15 April 1452 in or near the little town of Vinci, nestling against the slopes of Monte Albano and a day's journey from the glittering city of Florence. He was the illegitimate son of a rising Florentine legal official, Ser Piero da Vinci. Although little is known of Leonardo's mother, Caterina, the boy was acknowledged cheerfully by Ser Piero and was brought up by him and Leonardo's step-mother.

Virtually nothing is known of Leonardo's childhood, though biographers have speculated on the theme of the young Leonardo in the green Tuscan countryside, acquiring his lifelong fascination with nature. Certainly he began drawing and painting at an early age. According to the 16th century artist and art historian Giorgio Vasari, Leonardo's work so impressed his father that he took samples into Florence to show his friend Andrea del Verrocchio, one of the leading

John Heseltine

## Key Dates

**1452** born in or near Vinci, Italy

**1469** apprenticed to Verrocchio in Florence

**1476** accused of sodomy

**c.1482** moves to Milan

**1483** commissioned for *Virgin of the Rocks*

**1493** completes clay model of *The Great Horse* for Ludovico Sforza, Duke of Milan

**1495** begins *The Last Supper*

**1499** Milan invaded by the French; Leonardo leaves for Venice and Florence

**1502-3** works as a military engineer for Cesare Borgia, then returns to Florence

**1506** returns to Milan

**1512-13** French expelled from Milan; moves to Rome

**1516-17** 'retires' to Amboise in France

**1519** dies in France

**The young Leonardo?** *(below) It is thought that the figure of St Michael from* Tobias and the Archangels, *attributed to Francesco Botticini (1445-97), is a likeness of Leonardo, who would have been about 18 when the picture was painted.*

Scala

Uffizi, Florence

artists of the day. Verrocchio was also enthusiastic, and Ser Piero enrolled his teenage son in the master's busy workshop.

Verrocchio's workshop, like that of other major artists, was something of a cross between an art school and a design studio. Apprentices such as Leonardo worked their way up from sweeping floors to mixing colours to helping out in the production of commissioned paintings. Leonardo had reached this stage by the age of 20, when Verrocchio gave him responsibility for painting one of the angels in *The Baptism of Christ* (c.1472).

Leonardo's angel radiated his youthful genius. Vasari wrote that Verrocchio 'never touched colours again, he was so ashamed that the boy understood their use better than he did'. Leonardo had 'graduated', and became a master of the painters' Guild of St Luke, which allowed him to set up as an independent painter. However, he remained based at Verrocchio's until the late 1470s.

Leonardo had learned a good deal, in the years that he spent at his master's studio, and not all of it

**Arno Landscape (1473)**
*(right) This pen drawing of the Arno valley is dated 1473 – or rather ЄҬҌӀ – in Leonardo's customary mirror-writing. The artist's first dated work, it was executed when he was 21 and working in Florence.*

Uffizi, Florence

Uffizi, Florence

from Verrocchio. Florence in the 15th century was one of the great cultural centres of the world, and Leonardo would have come into contact with many of the scholars whose new ideas and learning were shaping the intellectual climate of Renaissance Italy. Most importantly of all, he would have known the renowned mathematician, geographer and astronomer Paolo Toscanelli. As Florence's most celebrated scholar, Toscanelli was sure to include among his house guests the best and brightest passing through the city.

## A DISTRUST OF SOCIETY

Somewhere about this time, Leonardo became a vegetarian. It was one of many ways in which he seemed to distance himself from his contemporaries. Not that he was a recluse – according to Vasari, 'Leonardo's disposition was so lovable that he commanded everyone's affection', and there are many other accounts of his good looks and charm, as well as his quirky sense of humour that gave him a lifelong taste for practical jokes. Yet he always had a deep distrust of human society: 'Alone you are all yourself,' he wrote, 'with a companion you are half yourself.'

The first years of Leonardo's life as a fully-fledged artist coincided with the rise of supreme power in Florence of Lorenzo de' Medici – 'il Magnifico'. He ruled the prosperous city-state

**Leonardo's angel**
*(above) Leonardo painted the left-hand angel in Verrocchio's* Baptism of Christ *while he was still an apprentice. The young artist's brilliance so astounded Verrocchio that – according to Vasari – he gave up painting.*

**The Bridges of Florence**
*(below) The Ponte Vecchio in the foreground was the first bridge to span the river Arno which runs through Florence and provided the source of energy for the profitable cloth industry.*

**The towers of Vinci**
*(above) Leonardo spent his childhood in the quiet hill town of Vinci, amid the rolling Tuscan countryside less than 20 miles from Florence. Two towers dominate the little town: that on the right belongs to the church where – according to local tradition – Leonardo was baptized; that on the left now houses a Leonardo museum.*

# Leonardo's Master

Although the fame of Andrea del Verrocchio (1435-88) has been overshadowed by that of his most brilliant pupil, Leonardo, he was a major artist in his own right. At the time when Leonardo entered his busy workshop, Verrocchio was the principal sculptor in Florence, and one of the most sought after artists in all Italy.

Trained as a goldsmith, Verrocchio's work is marked by its exquisite craftsmanship. And though he practised mainly as a sculptor, he also excelled in engraving and painting. His reputation attracted some of the most promising young artists to his studio, including Pietro Perugino who later became the master of the great painter Raphael.

Ufhzi, Florence

Bargello, Florence

**Portrait of Verrocchio**
*(left) This portrait of the master has been attributed to one of his pupils, Lorenzo di Credi. Though Verrocchio's real surname was di Cione, the name by which he is known means 'true eye' – a reflection of his esteemed reputation as an artist.*

**The virile and the effeminate**
*(above and left) These two sculptures by Verrocchio show the two different 'types' of men which also appear in Leonardo's art. In* The Colleoni Monument, *the feeling of brute power and restrained energy which emanates from the statue is topped by the rider's sneering face with its deep-cut lines and furrowed brow. A completely different feeling characterizes the figure of* David *(detail, left) – with his delicate features and enigmatic half-smile.*

with shrewd self-interest, and like many members of his family had cultivated tastes. Yet Leonardo received little of the lavish patronage which abounded in Florence at the time: though he sketched obsessively, in the years he remained in Florence after leaving Verrocchio's studio, he executed – as far as is known – only a handful of paintings. The most important of these, *The Adoration of the Magi*, was left unfinished.

Part of the reason for this surprising lack of official work was that Leonardo, talented though he was, had probably already gained a reputation for not delivering his commissions. Once he had solved the problem of a composition, he tended to lose interest and was ready to move on to the next intellectual puzzle.

But he also had more wordly things on his mind. In 1476, he was twice accused of the crime of sodomy, though both charges were dismissed through lack of evidence. It may well be that he was homosexual – he never married, and later in life usually contrived to have a young man or two about him – but it seems more likely that there was little room in his life for sexual relationships with

The Sforza Altarpiece (detail)/Brera, Milan

Leonardo/Portrait of an Old man and a Youth/Uffizi, Florence

**The city of Milan**
*(above) Leonardo spent over 20 years of his life in Milan in northern Italy just south of the Alps. Although it boasted the largest cathedral in the country, Milan lagged far behind Florence in both architecture and culture. But it was immensely rich – with thriving textile and arms industries.*

either men or women. He distrusted passion of any sort other than intellectual.

And Leonardo's intellectual pursuits were widespread to say the least. Although he despised the violent politics of Medici's Florence, he spent a fair amount of his time in the late 1470s designing a whole armoury of murderous engines, including a primitive machine gun. He was soon to use his ingenuity in this field in an attempt to gain favour – and employment – from one of Medici's rivals, Ludovico Sforza, the ruthless Duke of Milan. Around 1482, Leonardo left Florence, and travelled to this northern city in search of work.

**The lovely Salai**
*(above) This curly haired young man is thought to be Leonardo's friend Salai. The grotesque features of the old man opposite him emphasize Salai's youthful beauty.*

His Milanese career got off to a slow start, but in 1483 he received an important commission from the Church of San Francesco Grande. The church's prior may have heard of Leonardo's reluctance to complete a piece of work for he drew up a lengthy contract which specified a seven-month deadline. He could have saved himself the trouble as the painting – *The Virgin of the Rocks* – was not delivered for another 25 years.

## A STATUE FOR THE DUKE

While work was beginning on *The Virgin of the Rocks*, Leonardo was already thinking about another – as yet only imagined – work of art. He knew that Duke Ludovico intended to honour his brigand father with a massive equestrian statue, and was determined to gain the commission. He sent the Duke an extraordinary letter in which he outlined his prowess as a military inventor and engineer. Among other startling claims, he declared that he could make bridges that were 'indestructible by fire and battle', and 'chariots, safe and unassailable'. Almost as an afterthought, he offered his services as an architect, a sculptor and a painter.

Leonardo's opportunings had the desired effect. In 1483, he was allowed to begin work on the Great Horse. His projected statue was an immense undertaking. Innovative as always, Leonardo was unwilling to produce the usual static sculpture: he set himself the seemingly impossible task of creating a 26 feet high rearing

The Sforza Altarpiece (detail)/Brera, Milan

**Duke Ludovico Sforza**
*(far left) Ludovico Sforza, the despotic ruler of Milan was nicknamed 'Il Moro' (The Moor) because of his dark complexion. He was a vain and boastful man who ruled his glittering court with an iron hand.*

**The Duke's child bride**
*(left) When Il Moro was 39, he married the 15-year-old Beatrice d'Este, whose family ruled the neighbouring city-state of Ferrara. The young duchess delighted in her extravagant life-style, and bore her husband a son when she was 17. But she died in childbirth a few years later.*

horse. Such a feat had never been achieved before, and much time was needed to solve the problem.

But Ludovico Sforza was not a patient man, and by 1489 he was writing to Florence in search of another sculptor who could get the work done more quickly. Meanwhile, Leonardo made himself a kind of Master of Revels at the Duke's court, designing stage machinery and amusing mechanical toys. When no sculptor could be found to take on the Great Horse project, Leonardo was authorized to resume work on it. By November 1493, the full-sized clay model was complete. All that was needed was for Sforza to assemble the 90-odd tons of bronze required for its casting.

While he was waiting for the bronze, Leonardo began work on a huge mural of *The Last Supper* for the nearby monastery church of Santa Maria delle Grazie. Its brilliance was indisputable, and even before it was finished, it drew many admiring pilgrims to the monastery. But Leonardo had used a disastrously experimental technique and within a few years his masterpiece was peeling off the damp wall of the monastery's refectory.

## SUCCESS AND ADMIRATION

At the time though, neither Leonardo nor his contemporaries knew what lay in store. At 42, he was at the peak of his career, admired and respected by all. He had his own school of apprentices, and had never been busier. Perhaps he fretted when he heard that Ludovico had sent the bronze once destined for the Great Horse to his embattled brother-in-law to make cannons. But there were brighter things to think of.

He had acquired a protégé – a young boy 'with lovely hair and lovely curls and well-shaped eyes and mouth', known as Salai. And he was writing his *Treatise on Painting*, a huge work which was to influence artists for centuries to come.

Leonardo's notebooks were filling rapidly, crammed with sketches and comments written in his precise, left-to-right, mirror-image hand. He could see nothing without wanting to study it: birds, plants, the movement of water. Above all, he became passionately interested in human anatomy, and increasingly involved with the grim but fascinating business of dissection. And what did not exist to observe, he could imagine. During these years came the first flood of inventions – a submarine, a tank, even a helicopter.

Leonardo continued to shower his patron with grandiose proposals for great works of architecture and civil engineering. He took up town planning, and produced a massive scheme for the rebuilding of all Milan, with airy boulevards and an impeccable sewage system. But Ludovico was rarely interested: by the end of the century, he was struggling to keep control of the city. In 1499, Milan fell to Louis XII of France.

With Ludovico and his court gone, there was nothing to keep Leonardo in Milan, and he left the city. But he had stayed just long enough to see the entry of Louis's army, and the destruction of a

# Leonardo's Drawings

Leonardo made hundreds of sheets of drawings, which display the universal nature of his interests. He used them primarily as an aid to scientific research, although their preoccupations are often reflected in his paintings. They were usually accompanied by observations in his famous mirror writing.

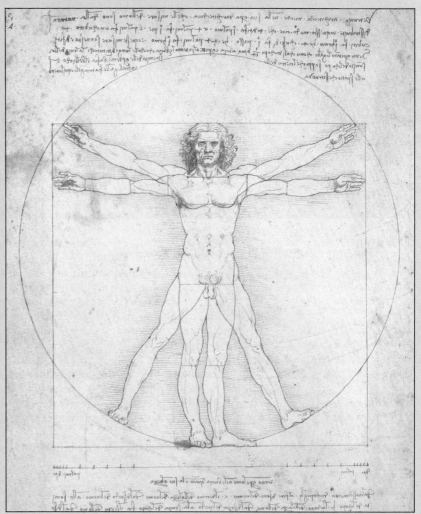

Illustration to Vitruvius's *De Architectura*/Accademia, Venice

**Flying machines** *(right) Leonardo spent more than 20 years of his life trying to devise a way for man to fly. He studied the flight of birds, bats and even insects, and invented a variety of ingenious machines. One of his most incredible contraptions was the 'aerial screw' – or helicopter – based on contemporary whirligig toys.*

Institut de France, Paris

Scala

**The Proportions of the Human Figure (c.1492)**
*(left) This famous drawing illustrates a passage from a Roman treatise on architecture, in which man is shown to be 'the measure of all things'.*

**Botanical drawings**
*(below) This study of crowfoot, star of Bethlehem, wood-anemone and leafy-branched spurge may have been connected with the lost painting of Leda.*

**Ideal architecture**
*(right) Leonardo made several drawings of ideal churches – none of which were ever built. He clearly delighted in playing elaborate games with geometric shapes.*

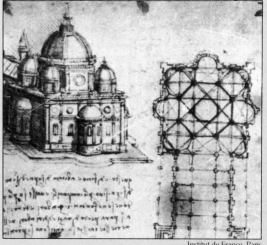

Institut de France, Paris

Reproduced by gracious permission of Her Majesty The Queen

Royal Library, Windsor

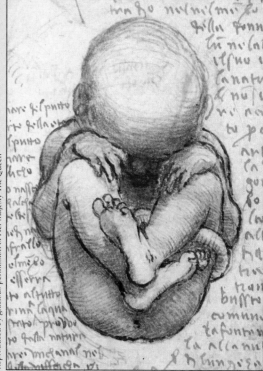

Reproduced by gracious permission of Her Majesty The Queen

Royal Library, Windsor

Ambrosiana, Milan

**Military devices**
*(left) Leonardo designed a whole range of war machines for Ludovico Sforza, including these deadly mortar bombs. The holes in the mortars meant that they exploded into fragments – a horribly practical idea. Leonardo assured Ludovico that if bombardment should fail he could 'contrive endless means of defence and offence'.*

**Anatomical studies**
*(above) When he was in his last years, Leonardo claimed that he had dissected over 30 bodies of men and women of all ages. He recorded his findings with scientific accuracy, and even planned a treatise on anatomy. His researches include an analysis of the human nervous system and a study of the position of the foetus in the womb.*

**The Battle of Anghiari**
(left) In 1503, Leonardo began work on a battle scene for Florence's council chamber. Working opposite him was his rival Michelangelo, who was depicting another scene, The Battle of Cascina. Michelangelo left his work unfinished. Leonardo used a disastrously experimental technique. All that remains of his great mural are drawings and copies like this one by Rubens.

**Leonardo's beneficiary**
(below) This young man has been identified as Francesco Melzi, whom Leonardo favoured in his will.

Louvre, Paris

personal dream. For during a week of drunken plunder, the French archers had found his huge clay model, and used it for target practice. His Great Horse was in ruins.

Accompanied by Salai, now a young man of about 20, Leonardo travelled east to Venice. He stayed only a few months, and soon turned his steps southwards to Florence, the home he had not seen for 18 years. In the interim, his reputation had rocketed, and he was received with respect, but it seems that he was not ready to settle in Florence. In 1502 he left the city, enlisting in the service of the infamous Cesare Borgia.

### BORGIA'S MILITARY ENGINEER

For Borgia was engaged in conquests in central Italy, and he needed a military engineer. Leonardo was the perfect choice – for apart from being the best brain in Italy, his respectability and renown would lend some credibility to Cesare's treacherous court. So for a few months in 1502-3, Leonardo wandered around Italy inspecting fortifications – and then suddenly shrugged off his connection with Borgia. He returned to Florence to live as an artist again.

It was a productive period for Leonardo. Around this time he produced the most celebrated of all his works – the *Mona Lisa*. But the other major work of this period turned out to be another technical disaster. In 1503, the government of Florence commissioned him to paint an epic picture of *The Battle of Anghiari*, to glorify an encounter in a war with Milan some 60 years before. As with *The Last Supper*, Leonardo used an experimental technique, the ruinous effects of which soon became obvious. The Florentines

Boltraffio/A Young Man/Gottfried Keller Collection/Kunstmuseum Bern

demanded that he either repair the painting or refund the payments they had made.

Typically, Leonardo ignored the demands. He was living in his villa in nearby Fiesole, drawing and sketching industriously, and was only rescued from some sort of legal action by the arrival of a gracious summons from the French Viceroy in Milan, Charles d'Amboise.

D'Amboise had no authority in the Florentine Republic, but the city had enemies enough without making more. So the Florentines parted

José Dupont/Explorer

**Retirement in France**
*(above) Leonardo spent his final years in the manor house of Clos-Lucé in the Loire valley. The house is now a Leonardo museum.*

with their artist, who was rapturously received in Milan. Anatomy became Leonardo's ruling passion once more: he was certain that his work would be of lasting benefit to humanity, and pushed himself accordingly.

But his life was not all work. In 1508, he found himself another protégé, a handsome young man named Francesco Melzi, whom he went so far as to adopt as his son. Perhaps, if it had been up to Leonardo, he would have passed the remainder of his life in Milan. But in 1512 an improbable alliance between the Swiss, the Spaniards, the Venetians and the papacy contrived to expel the French from Milan and install as Duke the son of Ludovico Sforza. Leonardo's comfortable world at the Viceroy's court had been shattered. At 61 years of age, he packed up his belongings, and – accompanied by Salai and Melzi – set off for Rome.

A new pope had just been elected – Leo X, the son of Lorenzo de' Medici. Leonardo had some hopes of exciting new commissions, and appears to have been in good spirits at first. But the pope had little time for him: Leonardo was yesterday's man now, with a string of uncompleted works and grandiose failures behind him. So when Francis I, successor to Louis XII of France, offered him a gentler oblivion as an honoured pensioner in a manor house close to the royal palace at Amboise, Leonardo accepted and moved to France.

Ageing, frail, and with his left hand partially paralyzed by a stroke, Leonardo fussed over his manuscripts, preparing them in a half-hearted way for publication. In one of his notebooks he had written: 'As a well-spent day brings happy sleep, so life well used brings happy death.' And quietly, on May 2 1519, a few weeks after his 67th birthday, Leonardo da Vinci died. The world had lost perhaps its most universal genius.

Reproduced by gracious permission of Her Majesty The Queen

Royal Library, Windsor

**An aged sage**
*(above) This drawing by Leonardo (c.1513) is sometimes thought to be a self-portrait. Certainly, the image of a world-weary old sage, contemplating his long life would have had much in common with Leonardo in his 60s.*

**The Death of Leonardo da Vinci**
*(right) This imaginative reconstruction was painted by the 19th century master Ingres. It shows the artist dying in the arms of King Francis I of France – an indication of the status which Leonardo had achieved.*

Bulloz

# Gallery

Leonardo trained in the studio of Andrea del Verrocchio and his earliest works, such as the exquisite Annunciation painted when he was about 20, reveal the superb standards of craftsmanship that he learned from his redoubtable master.

Throughout his life, religious works vied with portraits as Leonardo's main subject.

The Lady with an Ermine shows the great strides he took as a portraitist in easy naturalism of pose and expression – Ginevra de' Benci, painted about ten years earlier, looks stiff in comparison. The Mona Lisa, Leonardo's most famous and familiar work, carries this subtlety still further.

In religious painting, Leonardo's achievement was diverse, ranging from the majesty of The Last Supper, which established the rhetorical 'grand manner' that became accepted as the norm for such subjects, to the tender intimacy of The Virgin and Child with St Anne, one of the most beautiful expressions of maternal love in the history of art.

**The Annunciation**
*c.1472*
38¾" × 85½"
Uffizi, Florence

*There is no documentary evidence concerning this painting, but it is of such high quality that most authorities consider it one of Leonardo's early masterpieces, probably painted soon after he became a master in the painters' guild in Florence. The exquisite 'carpet' of flowers reveals all Leonardo's love of botanical detail, and the angel's wings are, with typical scientific curiosity, modelled on those of a bird.*

**Ginevra de' Benci** *c.1474*
15¾″ × 14½″ National Gallery, Washington

*Leonardo probably painted this picture to mark the wedding of Ginevra de' Benci, the daughter of a friend. The foliage framing her head is that of a juniper tree (in Italian 'ginepra') – a punning reference to her name. The sitter looks rather sullen, but Leonardo conveys great individuality of personality.*

**Lady with an Ermine** *c.1485*
21¾″ × 15¾″ Czartoryski Museum, Cracow

*This wonderfully graceful portrait probably represents Cecilia Gallerani, the mistress of Ludovico Sforza. An ermine was one of Ludovico's emblems, and the Greek word for the animal – 'galen' – is a pun on Cecilia's surname. Her attentive gaze and the ermine's predatory expression are painted with equal mastery.*

**The Last Supper** *c.1495-97*
166″ × 355″ Santa Maria delle Grazie, Milan

*In spite of its battered condition, Leonardo's only surviving mural retains much of the dignified authority that made it the most revered painting in the world. He shows the moment when Christ tells his disciples that one of them will betray him, their varied reactions depicted with unprecedented psychological subtlety.*

**The Virgin and Child with St Anne and John the Baptist** *c.1499*
54¾″ × 41″ National Gallery, London

*For several years Leonardo was intrigued by this subject, which
presented a great challenge to his skill in grouping figures. This
wonderfully tender chalk drawing was a cartoon for a painting that was
never executed; he later did a similar painting (p.29), but without
the figure of St John.*

**The Virgin of the Rocks** *c.1508*
74½″ × 47¼″ National Gallery, London

*This is the second of two versions of the subject by Leonardo, and it is
unclear why an artist who finished so little should repeat himself. He
was still working on this picture in 1508, but it may have been
started much earlier. Some parts may be by a studio assistant, but the
finest passages are of superlative quality.*

**Mona Lisa (La Gioconda)** *c.1503*
30¼″ × 20¾″ Louvre, Paris

*This portrait of Lisa Gherardini, wife of the Florentine merchant
Francesco di Zanobi del Giocondo, is now so famous that it is hard to
appreciate how original the pose and expression were in their
naturalism and subtlety. Leonardo is said to have employed musicians
and jesters to keep Mona Lisa amused as he worked.*

**The Virgin and Child with St Anne** *c.1510*
66½″ × 51¼″ Louvre, Paris

*This is Leonardo's final version of a favourite theme. Although unfinished, it has some breathtaking passages and shows Leonardo's incomparable skill with* sfumato – *the blending of tones so subtly that they merge, in his own words, 'without lines or borders in the manner of smoke'.*

# 'Motions of the Mind'

**As a painter, Leonardo wanted to represent not only appearances but also feelings – 'the motions of the mind'. This approach changed the status of the great artist from craftsman to genius.**

In his *Lives of the Artists*, first published in 1550, Giorgio Vasari wrote that Leonardo's 'name and fame will never be extinguished'. The claim has been borne out by posterity, for Leonardo is one of the few artists whose reputation has never wavered from his own lifetime to the present day. His contemporaries thought his talent was little less than divine, and in the centuries since his death, painters, poets and philosophers have looked to him as a shining example of the heights to which the human mind and spirit can attain.

Leonardo's surviving artistic output seems a remarkably thin platform for such widespread and lustrous fame. Scarcely a dozen paintings are universally accepted as being from his own hand, and of these several are unfinished or damaged.

Leonardo's achievement, then, is of an altogether exceptional kind, for although he began

Károly Szelényi/Corvina Archives, Budapest

Museum of Fine Arts, Budapest

**Leonardo the sculptor**
*Although Leonardo spent much of his time working on sculptural projects, there is no surviving piece of sculpture that is unquestionably from his own hand. This marvellously spirited bronze horse and rider has the best claim to be considered an authentic work by him. It has an energy and a mastery of equine anatomy typical of Leonardo, and is related in style to his* Battle of Anghiari *mural.*

comparatively few major works, and finished even fewer, he has imposed himself on the consciousness of artists and critics (and even the general public) in a way that only a handful of other cultural giants can match. This seeming paradox is explained not simply by the wonderful quality of the few paintings Leonardo did bring to fruition, but also by the revolution in attitudes towards art that he brought about. Virtually single-handed, Leonardo created the idea of the artist as genius. Earlier painters had achieved wealth, fame and position, but they were still regarded essentially as craftsmen, for in the Middle Ages and early Renaissance the visual arts were not considered to be on the same intellectual plane as literature or music.

## THE PAINTER-PHILOSOPHER

To Leonardo, the art of painting lay as much in the head as in the hands, and after him it was no more possible to judge a painting by the costliness of its materials than it was to judge a piece of music by the number of notes it contained or a poem by its number of words. Leonardo believed that painting was superior to any other art, and he presented his case ingeniously; people make

**A patient draughtsman**
*Leonardo often made elaborate drapery studies for his paintings – this detail of one was probably for* The Annunciation *(p.20). Vasari tells us that Leonardo 'would make clay models of figures, draping them with soft rags dipped in plaster and then draw them patiently'.*

Corsini Gallery, Rome/Bridgeman Art Library

pilgrimages to see great paintings, he argued, but no-one travels miles to read a poem. And to him the clinching argument in favour of the visual arts was that anyone would rather lose their hearing than their sight. He thought that painting was superior to sculpture in that the latter involves hard, noisy and messy physical labour, whereas the painter could wear fine clothes and listen to music or poetry as he worked.

Leonardo's fascination with the intellectual problems of art is one reason why his drawings so outnumber his paintings. He thought that the painter had to represent two main things: man and 'the motions of man's mind'. The first part – the naturalistic representation of appearances – was, to Leonardo, straightforward; the second part – the revelation of character through gesture and expression – was more difficult.

Once Leonardo had solved the problems of composition and characterization in his drawings, completing the job – the mere exercise of technical skill – held little appeal. He infuriated his paymasters by putting things off, and his failure to complete *The Virgin of the Rocks* for the church in Milan that had commissioned it led to a law suit.

When he could bring himself to finish a picture, however, Leonardo outshone even the greatest of his contemporaries. Oil painting was at that time a fairly new technique in Italy and Leonardo was

**Portrait of a Musician (c.1490)**
*This unfinished picture is Leonardo's only surviving male portrait. The attribution to Leonardo is disputed by some authorities, but the exquisitely curling hair, elegant fingers and air of intellectual intensity are worthy of the master. Leonardo himself was a skilful musician.*

Ambrosiana, Milan

**St Jerome (c.1480)**
*(below) It is not known for whom Leonardo painted this picture or why he left it unfinished. Leonardo's understanding of anatomy shows clearly in the thoroughly convincing portrayal of the ascetic saint's sinewy body.*

Bibliotheque Royale, Turin

**Left-handed shading**
*(above) Leonardo was left-handed, and this silverpoint drawing shows his distinctive left-handed shading. A right-handed artist instinctively shades with lines going from right down to left, but a left-handed draughtsman shades in the reverse.*

Vatican Picture Gallery, Rome/Scala

one of the first great masters of it. To a profoundly thoughtful worker like him, slow-drying oil paints were the ideal medium, allowing him to make infinitely subtle gradations of tone and to paint details such as plants and rocks with an exquisite precision that would gladden the heart of a botanist or a geologist.

Leonardo wanted to attain the same beauty of finish when he painted murals, so he rejected the time-honoured fresco technique, which demanded great swiftness in execution. His experiments to find a suitable alternative were disastrous; *The Last Supper,* painted in a kind of tempera, began to peel off the wall in his lifetime, and *The Battle of Anghiari* ran down the wall when the paint failed to dry (he was trying to imitate a technique described by the Roman writer Pliny).

## THE MASTER DRAUGHTSMAN

With the exception of *The Battle of Anghiari,* almost all Leonardo's paintings were either religious subjects or portraits. His drawings, however, cover an astonishing range of subjects, for he used them not only as preparation for his paintings, but also as an essential tool in his scientific research. He was the most prolific draughtsman of his time and used a wide variety of media, notably pen, chalk and silverpoint, in which the artist draws with a fine silver wire on specially prepared paper. The silver produces extraordinarily delicate lines, but the technique needs great sureness as erasure is impossible.

The sheer variety of Leonardo's interests was the main reason why he finished so little in his primary vocation of painting. Apart from his manifold scientific pursuits, he was also a sculptor and an architect. No work that is indisputably his survives in either medium, but his ideas and expertise were important in both fields.

The splendid bronze group of *St John the Baptist between a Pharisee and a Levite* over the north door of the Baptistery in Florence, for example, is the work of Giovanni Francesco Rustici, but Leonardo played a major role in its creation. Vasari tells us

Louvre, Paris

**The Virgin of the Rocks (c.1483)**
*(above) This is the earlier of two versions of the subject that Leonardo painted. The strange rocks that create the grotto setting (detail, above right) are a common feature in Leonardo's work. He was passionately interested in geology, which to him was part of the mystery of creation.*

**A study in perspective**
*Leonardo made this complex perspective drawing as a preparatory study for* The Adoration of the Magi. *The lines have been drawn in silverpoint, using a rule, and the figures are drawn on top in ink.*

Uffizi, Florence

TRADEMARKS

# The Pointing Finger

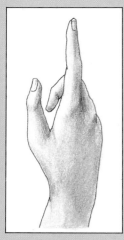

A figure with an enigmatic pointing finger often occurs in Leonardo's work. The finger usually points upwards, but in *The Virgin of the Rocks* the angel points emphatically at the infant John the Baptist. Whatever its significance for Leonardo, the gesture now evokes a sense of mystery.

Réunion des Musées Nationaux

that Rustici 'would allow no one near save Leonardo, who never left him while he was moulding and casting until the work was finished'. In architecture, Leonardo's designs for 'ideal' churches were influential on his friend Bramante, the greatest architect of the High Renaissance, and the ingenious double spiral staircase at the château of Chambord probably derives from an idea of his.

Leonardo's influence was spread also by his writings. His notes were gathered together and published as his *Treatise on Painting* in 1651, but they had wide circulation even before then. The few paintings that he left to posterity (or that survived long enough to be copied and re-copied) had an unprecedented effect on succeeding artists. Indeed, Leonardo's influence has been so great that it is harder to think of major painters who do not owe something to him than of those who do.

COMPARISONS

# Landscapes of the Imagination

Landscape painting did not become established as an independent subject of art until the 17th century. But painters before then often made telling use of landscape backgrounds or settings, naturalistic or imaginative. Mantegna was one of the greatest Italian painters of the generation before Leonardo. His style is strong and hard-edged, and although his rockscape reveals an imaginative power comparable to Leonardo's, it does not have the latter's sense of mystery. Landscape played a comparatively small part in the wide-ranging genius of Rembrandt, the greatest Dutch artist of the 17th century, but he brought to it his own sense of brooding intensity.

National Gallery, London

**Andrea Mantegna** (c.1430-1506)
**The Agony in the Garden**
*(above) Mantegna depicts Christ in anguish as he prays in the Garden of Gethsemane during the night before his Crucifixion. The sharp-edged rocks create emotional tension.*

**Rembrandt van Rijn** (1606-69)
**Stormy Landscape**
*(below) Rembrandt created drama in his landscapes less by the subject he depicted than by his forceful handling of light and shade. His half-defined forms loom from mysterious shadows.*

Herzog Anton Ulrich Museum, Brunswick

## THE MAKING OF A MASTERPIECE

# The Last Supper

*The Last Supper* was painted for the refectory (dining-room) of the monastery of Santa Maria delle Grazie in Milan. Leonardo probably took about three years on the work, from 1495 to 1498. The time-honoured method for wall-painting was fresco, but Leonardo rejected this for a more flexible technique using paints that would normally be applied to a wooden panel.

The process proved unstable and the painting soon began to peel off the wall. Vasari recorded that 'the prior was puzzled by Leonardo's habit of sometimes spending half a day at a time contemplating what he had done so far', but when he complained Leonardo explained that 'men of genius sometimes accomplish most when they work the least, for they are thinking out inventions and forming in their minds the perfect idea that they subsequently express with their hands.'

Scala

Enrico Ferrorelli/Dot/Colorific!

By gracious permission of Her Majesty The Queen

Royal Library, Windsor

**A study for St James**
(*above*) *Leonardo made several beautiful drawings for individual heads in* The Last Supper, *and this red chalk study for St James the Greater (fifth from the right in the painting) is one of the finest. In the lower part of the sheet is an architectural study – Leonardo's mind was always wandering.*

# Restoring a masterpiece

**Restoration in progress**
(*left*) *The Last Supper began to decay in Leonardo's lifetime, and some 50 years after the artist's death Vasari described it as 'so badly preserved that one can see only a muddle of dots'. It was first restored in 1726, and since then there have been numerous attempts to repair or preserve it, some doing more harm than good. The restoration at present in progress may take five years to complete.*

Enrico Ferrorelli/Dot/Colorific!

**Infinite patience**
(*right*) *Sometimes spending a day on an area the size of a postage stamp, the restorer is cleaning off almost five centuries of dirt, mould and overpaint. In some areas of the picture none of Leonardo's original paint survives.*

Santa Maria delle Grazie, Milan

Accademia, Venice

### Planning the composition
*(above) One of Leonardo's preliminary drawings for* The Last Supper *shows that he originally thought of separating Judas from the other figures on the near side of the table. He rejected this as too crude.*

### The monks' dining-room
*(below) The Last Supper was a highly appropriate subject for a dining-room and was often chosen for the refectory of a monastery. The refectory at Santa Maria delle Grazie was newly built when Leonardo painted his mural, which covers one of the end walls of the building.*

> 'That figure is most praiseworthy which by its action best conveys the passions of the soul.'
>
> Leonardo da Vinci

### Groups of three
*(above) Leonardo has arranged the twelve disciples into four groups of three. The composition is so skilful and fluent that it is rarely noticed that he has taken liberties with the spacing. The disciples are so tightly packed that they could not possibly all have been sitting down together.*

Mike McGuinness

35

# The Borgias

**In Leonardo's time, Italy was a collection of independent states, ruled by rival families. The most famous of these were the Borgias, infamous for their political intrigue and treachery.**

Leonardo first met Cesare Borgia in 1499 when the notorious adventurer accompanied Louis XII of France on his invasion of Milan, ruled at the time by Leonardo's patron Ludovico Sforza. Borgia was a fascinating figure – an exquisitely dressed and handsome young man who knew how to charm, despite his reputation for audacity, cruelty and licentiousness. He soon realized that Leonardo's extraordinary genius as inventor and engineer would be invaluable to him in his military campaigns, and later invited him to become his military engineer and architect.

Leonardo was in Borgia's service from the summer of 1502 to February 1503, designing fortifications, inventing weapons and preparing military maps as he moved with the army through the Romagna, to the east and north-east of Florence. In his notebooks, Leonardo makes no reference at all to the appalling acts of violence committed all round him during those months.

Leonardo would certainly have been aware that three members of the Borgia family – Cesare, his sister Lucrezia and his father Pope Alexander VI – were widely accused of treachery, murder, torture and incest. Some of these accusations may have been fabricated, or at any rate exaggerated, in rumours started by the family's many enemies. The Borgias were isolated by their Spanish origins and were resented in particular by the powerful Roman families of Orsini and Colonna.

## THE RISE OF A DYNASTY

Alexander VI was born Rodrigo de Borja in 1431 in Valencia, Spain, – the name was later Italianized. His uncle, Pope Calixtus III, made him a cardinal, and by the time he received the Keys of St Peter – amid charges of simony – the family was immensely wealthy. In many ways Alexander was an able administrator, but he continued to hand

Pinturicchio/La Disputa di Santa Caterina (detail)/Borgia Apartments, Vatican

**The papal city**
*(left) By the 15th century, Rome had established itself as the Holy City, and the Vatican had become the official residence of the pope. The basilica of St Peter's was situated alongside.*

Pinturicchio/Pope Alexander VI (detail)/Borgia Apartments, Vatican

**Vannozza dei Catanei**
*(above) A Roman lady renowned for her charm, Vannozza was Rodrigo Borgia's mistress for about 11 years, and the mother of Cesare, Juan and Luzcrezia.*

**Pope Alexander VI**
*(left) Rodrigo Borgia was elected pope on 11 August, 1492, amid widespread charges of corruption. A striking libertine and an able and unscrupulous politician, he pursued a ruthless campaign to secure his family's aggrandisement.*

**The pope's frescos**
*(left) This fresco is one of a series commissioned by Pope Alexander VI to decorate the Borgia apartment in the Vatican. The painting shows Catherine of Alexandria disputing with the pagan emperor Maximus. Lucrezia and Cesare were probably the models for Saint Catherine and the emperor, while the mounted horseman in the foreground is thought to be Juan. In the background, the Borgia bull presides over the occasion from the top of a triumphal arch.*

out important Church positions to relatives and supporters, while weakening his enemies through confiscation of their property and, it is assumed, by arranging for their 'liquidation' whenever this was necessary.

Alexander had fathered about seven children while still a cardinal and at least one other when he was pope, but it was not uncommon for clerics to have sexual relations with women and acknowledge broods of illegitimate offspring. In fact, if Alexander had a saving grace, it was his boundless affection for his children, particularly for Cesare, Juan and Lucrezia – all by Vannozza dei Catanei, who was his mistress for about 11 years.

The pope's devotion to his beautiful fair-haired daughter prompted scandalous tales of incest, and there was also speculation about relations between Lucrezia and Cesare. Alexander's fondness did not, however, prevent him from arranging a succession of marriages solely in order to cement ties with whichever political ally he happened to need at the time.

Lucrezia's first betrothal, to a Spanish nobleman when she was 11, was annulled to allow a more useful marriage two years later to Giovanni Sforza of Milan. When that political alliance no longer served a purpose, the pope ended the marriage by forcing the unfortunate young husband into a public declaration which implied he was impotent. To strengthen links with the House of Aragon, which ruled the Kingdom of Naples, Lucrezia was married in 1498 to Alfonso, Duke of Bisceglie. By chance, this was a truly happy love match.

Just over two years later, Alfonso was brutally attacked outside the Vatican by a group of unknown assailants. Although he seemed to be recovering from his injuries, some days later he suddenly and mysteriously died. Most reports implicated Cesare, who was said to have called in his personal assassin to kill Alfonso, perhaps out of envy or jealousy over Lucrezia.

Within a month Alexander was seeking a new husband and decided on Alfonso d'Este, heir to the Dukedom of Ferrara. Lucrezia now left Rome for good, and, as custom dictated, parted from her much-loved first child Rodrigo.

Meanwhile Cesare, an archdeacon from the age of 7 and a cardinal from 17, had seized the long-awaited opportunity of throwing off his clerical

**Lucrezia Borgia**
(right) Alexander's favourite daughter was reputed to be a graceful fair-haired girl who was warm-hearted and generous. A victim of her father's scheming and her brother's possessive love, she outlived her Borgia notoriety and devoted herself to good works.

**The Borgia arms**
(above) At Alexander's coronation, the Borgia arms – a bull grazing in a gold field – lined the route of the procession. It later became a hated symbol of the tyrannical Borgia dynasty.

**Il Valentino**
(right) In some ways Cesare was a magnificent example of Renaissance man – handsome, bold and intelligent, but his ruthlessness and treachery made him feared and hated throughout Italy.

Accademia Carrara, Bergamo

Bartolommeo Veneto/Portrait of a Lady/National Gallery, London

robes and becoming a soldier. When Alexander's first son had died at a young age, his Spanish title, Duke of Gandia, had passed to the third son Juan, because Cesare, as the second born, had from birth been destined for the Church. When in 1497 Juan was stabbed to death and his body thrown into the River Tiber, Cesare was regarded by many as the prime suspect, although no proof was available.

At any rate it enabled Cesare to take over his murdered brother's coveted position of Captain-General of the Papal Troops, which the pope conferred on him after releasing him from his vows. Cesare also acquired the French title of Duke of Valentinois – the origin of Il Valentino, the name often used for him – in return for the pope's annulment of the French King's first marriage and dispensation for his second. While visiting France in 1498, Cesare married the French princess Charlotte d'Albret, by whom he had a daughter, but whom he quickly abandoned.

Italy at this time was a patchwork of independent states, the most important of which were Venice, Milan, Florence, the Spanish-ruled Kingdom of Naples, covering the southern part of the country, and the Papal States, which stretched diagonally across the centre. The north-eastern end of the Papal territories, the Romagna, was effectively ruled by a number of local barons, notable mainly for their greed and incompetence. Cesare's task was ostensibly to bring the Romagna firmly back under Papal rule; in fact it was a means

of gaining Italian lands and the title of Duke of Romagna for himself. One by one the towns fell to Cesare as he disposed of all opposition through trickery and assassination and by terrifying the populace into obedience. Even the well-administered duchies of Urbino and Camerino, loyal to the pope, did not escape.

## AN 'IDEAL' RULER

In Niccolò Machiavelli's book *The Prince*, written in 1513, Cesare Borgia is presented as an example of a supremely successful soldier and statesman. Machiavelli had met Il Valentino on at least two occasions when he was on diplomatic missions as Second Chancellor of the Florentine Republic.

Machiavelli stressed that Il Valentino's achievements would not have been possible without good fortune on his side. This fortune deserted Cesare in August 1503 when the pope died, leaving him without protection.

Alexander had fallen ill after dining at Cardinal Adrian's villa and it was widely believed that he had been poisoned by a potion which he had intended for the cardinal. The more likely cause of death was malaria, which was rife in the city that summer.

Cesare too was stricken, and this hampered his desperate plans to secure the election of the 'right' pope. Pius III was a reasonably safe choice, but died within a few weeks, and Cesare was unable to

prevent the subsequent election of Julius II, an enemy of the Borgias.

Cesare was forced to flee to Naples, but the Spanish rulers, anxious not to antagonize the new pope, sent him to Spain where he was imprisoned. After two years, Cesare made a characteristically daring escape and found his way to the French court of his brother-in-law Jean de Navarre, who made him captain of his mercenary troops. Cesare was killed at the siege of Viana in Navarre, on 12 March 1507, aged 31.

Lucrezia lived for another 12 years, dying at 39 of complications following childbirth. Her life in Ferrara must have been sad and lonely, for her husband had always regarded her with cold indifference. She relieved the tedium with romantic attachments to the poet Pietro Bembo and her brother-in-law Francesco Gonzaga, but contemporary reports also refer to her charitable works and the amount of respect she had earned from her subjects.

Stories of the Borgias' monstrous depravity and cruelty have crystallized into a semblance of truth through repeated telling, but most cannot actually be proved true. The family's deeds must in any case be viewed against the prevailing morality of an age in which nepotism, political assassinations, sexual promiscuity and street violence were commonplace. The Renaissance, with its unparalleled flowering of arts and learning, was in many other ways a monstrous time in which to rule or be ruled.

Palazzo Vecchio, Florence

**Niccolò Machiavelli**
*(left) Machiavelli spent several months with Cesare Borgia in the Autumn of 1502, as an emissary of the Florentine republic. He greatly admired Cesare's combination of audacity and diplomacy, and saw in him the qualities of leadership needed to unify the squabbling Italian states. During this time Machiavelli also met Leonardo. The two men were drawn together by their intellect, and became close friends.*

Dosso Dossi/A Bacchanal/National Gallery, London

© BBC

**Cesare's swift vengeance**
*(above) This scene from the television series* The Borgias *shows the execution of two of the condottieri who conspired against Cesare Borgia in 1502.*

**A patroness of the arts**
*(left) As Duchess of Ferrara, Lucrezia presided over a distinguished court. The painter Dosso Dossi was one of many artists who benefited from her patronage.*

# A Year in the Life 1492

**Italy faced troublesome years ahead as the death of Lorenzo de' Medici threw the nation's political system off balance and paved the way for an invasion by the French. That August, in Rome, Rodrigo Borgia became pope and Christopher Columbus put out to sea to set foot in the New World just over two months later.**

In April 1492, Lorenzo de' Medici, the powerful and highly-respected ruler of Leonardo's native Florence, lay dying. When lightning struck the cathedral dome, the extraordinary Dominican preacher, Girolamo Savonarola took it for an omen, thundering at his congregation 'Behold the sword of the Lord, swift and sure over the peoples of the earth!' And he warned the Florentines that terrible times lay ahead for the church and the state.

## A STRIFE-TORN ITALY

Savonarola's prophecies of doom were soon fulfilled. In Florence itself, Lorenzo's successor, his son Piero, showed none of his father's political tact or acumen, and under Savonarola's influence the city was soon subjected to a

Mauro Pucciarelli

Medici Museum, Florence

**Lorenzo the Magnificent**
*Like his father Cosimo (1389-1464), Lorenzo de' Medici was a wily politician and a generous patron of the arts. He was an accomplished writer and poet and did much to nurture Italian literature. Thanks to his political machinations, Lorenzo was able to exert a benign tyranny over Florence, during which she and the Medici family prospered. It was said that if Florence was to have a tyrant, she could never have found a better or more pleasant one. Lorenzo died on 8 April, aged 43.*

**Prophet of heavenly wrath**
*(right) Girolamo Savonarola (1452-1498) in his cell in the convent of San Marco in Florence. In 1492 he refused absolution to Lorenzo de' Medici thereby consigning his soul to hell, and prophesied famine, bloodshed and pestilence as a consequence of the Borgia papacy. Eventually the people of Florence grew tired of Savonarola's strictures, and willingly colluded with Pope Alexander VI in celebrating the execution of Savonarola and his adherents.*

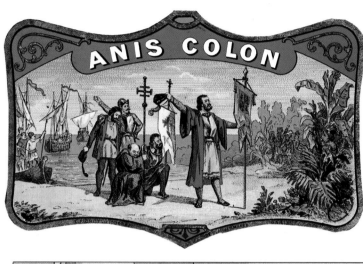

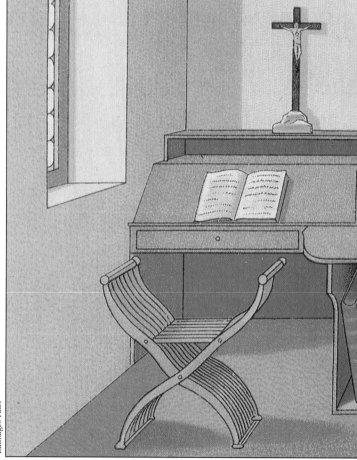

Edimages-Palix

fanatically harsh, hell-fearing régime. More important still, the death of Lorenzo destabilized Italian politics. A reshuffling of alliances led to the diplomatic isolation of Leonardo's master, Ludovico Sforza, who was so alarmed that he began making friendly overtures to the French king, Charles VIII. The subsequent French invasion (which Savonarola had uncannily predicted) unleashed a series of Italian wars, that was eventually to cost Ludovico his duchy and Leonardo his comfortable position at court – and was to make an impotent Italy the battleground of the great powers for years to come.

In Rome, that August, the Spanish-born cardinal Rodrigo Borgia was elected Pope, taking the title of Alexander VI. The reputation of the Borgia family has been unsavoury for centuries, though it is questionable whether they were much worse than many other Italian politicians and ecclesiastics in that amoral age. Alexander certainly fathered at least seven children, accumulated vast wealth, and bribed his way to the papal throne. Once in power, he did everything he could to advance his children, and his ruthless son Cesare Borgia had a brilliant but brief career as a despot and conqueror, employing Leonardo da Vinci as a military engineer and architect.

## QUEST FOR THE INDIES

On 3 August 1492, three Spanish vessels left the Atlantic port of Palos and headed out into the ocean towards the Canary Islands. The ships were the *Santa Maria*, the *Niña* and the *Pinta*; the commander of the modest expedition was an Italian sailor,

**Christopher Columbus**
*(left) The intrepid explorer, known by his Spanish employers as Cristóbal Colón (1451-1506). He left the Canary Islands and the known world on 6 September 1492, in quest, as he thought, of Japan. After sailing westwards for over a month, he and his three ships arrived at an island they named San Salvador on 12 October.*

Lauros-Giraudon

Musée des Beaux Arts, Dijon

**A Borgia with powers eternal**
*As a result of judicious bribery, Rodrigo Borgia (1431-1503) was elected Pope in 1492, taking the name Alexander VI. From this eminence he wielded a potent political influence throughout Europe, and honoured at least 30 of his relatives, including his illegitimate children, with lucrative high church offices. During his papacy he conducted an open liaison with his mistress, the beautiful Giulia Farnese, and fathered yet another child with an unknown woman.*

**Santa Maria delle Grazie, Milan**
*Donato d'Angelo Bramante (1444-1514) erected the cupola (shown below) and choir of Santa Maria delle Grazie in 1492. His work embodied the High Renaissance ideals of proportion and harmony. Bramante then went on to Rome to work on St. Peter's, which he also envisaged capped with a central dome.*

Scala

Christopher Columbus of Genoa (1451-1506); and its object was to find a route to 'the Indies' – the Far East – by travelling westward across the Atlantic.

Columbus was as much a visionary as Leonardo, but he was also a proud and audacious man with a single fixed idea. It had taken him ten years to find backers for his 'Enterprise of the Indies', despite the fact that many scholars were already convinced that the earth was round. The question remained: were the Indies too far to reach by ship? Columbus had calculated that they lay about 3,900 miles by sea from the Canaries – but he was quite wrong. He never dreamed that he would find an unknown continent and another vast ocean, the Pacific, between the Atlantic and the East.

On leaving the Canaries, Columbus's ships were driven along by strong and steady following winds. They made such good progress that, when briefing the crew, Columbus deliberately underestimated the distances covered, fearing that his men might panic when they realized how far from land they were. Even so, after 30 days they had had enough; and eventually, faced with the prospect of a mutiny, Columbus was forced to agree that he would turn back if no land appeared on the horizon within a few days. But at 2.00 in the morning on 12 October 1492, the look-out on the *Pinta* sighted an island – one of the Bahamas – and at dawn Columbus and his men set foot in the New World. Columbus claimed the land for King Ferdinand and Queen Isabella of Spain, and planted a royal standard on the shore. He did not know – and never was to know – that he had found the Americas.

Jacques Alexandre/The Image Bank

Vivien Fifield

### The birth of printing in England

*(left) This illustration is The Toll-Gatherer from 'Game of Chess' printed by William Caxton (c.1422-1492). His printing apprenticeship took place in Cologne, and in 1476 he returned to England and set up a press at the sign of the Red Pale in the City of Westminster. He was a tireless worker, and by his death he had published about 100 varied items including Chaucer's* Canterbury Tales *and Malory's* Morte d'Arthur.

### The end of Mohammedan rule

*(above) After ten years of bitter fighting, the Moorish kingdom of Granada, ruled by Abu Abdallah, finally fell to Ferdinand and Isabella of Spain on 2 January, 1492. This paved the way for the fanatical royal couple to subject the citizens of Granada to the horrors of the Inquisition, and incidentally gave Spain the military prowess which enabled her to win resounding victories throughout Europe for over a century.*

Jacopino del Conte/Portrait of Michelangelo/Casa Buonarroti, Florence

# MICHAELAGLVS·BONAROVS·

## 1475-1564

Michelangelo is one of the greatest artists who ever lived: his astonishing career encompasses the arts of painting, sculpture, architecture and even poetry. A proud citizen of Florence, he was determined from the first to raise the status of his family by virtue of his art. His ambition was soon fulfilled when he was taken into the household of Lorenzo de' Medici.

Michelangelo's reputation preceded him and he subsequently travelled to Rome, lured by prestigious commissions. Here he painted the celebrated Sistine Ceiling frescoes for his most formidable patron, Pope Julius II. Despite his fame, Michelangelo was a sad, highly sensitive and solitary figure. He died at the age of 89 and was buried, with great pomp, in Florence.

# The Divine Michelangelo

**A native of Florence, Michelangelo spent much of his long life in Rome, working for the popes. His creative powers and the diversity of his skills earned him the epithet 'divine'.**

Michelangelo di Ludovico Buonarroti Simoni (known as Michelangelo) was born on 6 March 1475 in the Tuscan town of Caprese, near Arezzo. His family were natives of Florence and they returned to the city within a few weeks of the birth, when Ludovico Buonarroti's term as mayor of Caprese had ended.

Soon after their arrival, the Buonarrotis sent the baby to a wet-nurse living on the family farm a few miles away in Settignano. This environment seems to have had a crucial effect on Michelangelo, for the area around Settignano was full of stone quarries. His wet-nurse's father and husband were both stonemasons, and Michelangelo often jested later in life that 'with my wet-nurse's milk, I sucked in the hammer and chisels I use for my statues'.

From an early age the young Michelangelo was consumed with artistic ambition. As a boy of 13, he persuaded his reluctant father to allow him to leave his grammar school and become an apprentice to the artist Domenico Ghirlandaio, one of the most successful fresco painters in Florence.

Michelangelo's remarkable gifts soon became apparent and, within a year or so, he was making pen line drawings that put his master's to shame. By 1489, Michelangelo was sent, along with a few of the best artists in Ghirlandaio's studio, to Lorenzo de' Medici's new 'sculpture school' in the Medici gardens. Here among the trees was one of the most impressive collections of ancient statuary

Private Collection/Bridgeman Art Library

**A formative influence** *(left) In April 1488 Michelangelo joined the workshop of Domenico Ghirlandaio, one of the finest Florentine fresco-painters of his day. At this time Ghirlandaio was engaged in the biggest commission of his career – a series of frescoes on the life of the Virgin and St John the Baptist in the church of Sta Maria Novella in Florence. As an apprentice, Michelangelo was probably involved in the work, and was introduced to the techniques of fresco painting.*

**The city of Florence** *(above) This view shows Florence in 1490, when Michelangelo was employed in the Medici household. Florence was also the Buonarroti family's native city.*

**An enlightened ruler** *(right) Widely respected for his skilful statesmanship, Lorenzo de' Medici was also a sensitive and intelligent man. A humanist poet and a great patron of the arts, he made his palace a home for leading philosophers and artists.*

Ghirlandaio/Birth of John the Baptist/Scala

in Italy, and under the watchful eye of the aged sculptor Bertoldo, Michelangelo began to copy and improve on these antique masterworks.

The young Michelangelo's prodigious skill – and, perhaps, his single-mindedness – soon aroused jealousy among his fellow students in the garden. His biographer and friend, Giorgio Vasari, tells of how another young sculptor, Pietro Torrigiano, later described as a bully, punched him violently in the face, crushing and breaking his nose. Michelangelo was deeply upset by the incident, and by the disfigurement to his face – physically, and psychologically, it seems to have 'marked him for life' (Vasari).

Michelangelo's skill now attracted the personal attention of Lorenzo de' Medici (called 'the Magnificent'), who was effective ruler of Florence at the time. He was so impressed by a statue Michelangelo was carving that he invited him to live in the Medici household.

## CHANGING FORTUNES

Michelangelo spent two happy years in the Medici household and worked on an impressive marble relief, *The Battle of the Centaurs*. But when Lorenzo died in 1492, Michelangelo's fortunes began to take a downward turn, and he went back to live with his father. Lorenzo's successor, Piero de' Medici, was friendly to the artist but had little interest in art. Indeed, the only work Piero commissioned from Michelangelo was a snowman, a childish whim after a heavy snowfall in January 1494. As a consolation, Michelangelo devoted his skills to a detailed study of anatomy by dissecting corpses in the church of Santo Spirito – a curious privilege bestowed by the prior in return for a carved wooden crucifix.

Under Piero's rather haphazard reign, political Florence became increasingly unstable and blood and thunder preachers found wide audiences. A charismatic Dominican called Savonarola had a

**The bully of the class**
*(above) Pietro Torrigiano was a fellow student of Michelangelo's in Bertoldo's sculpture class. During a sketching expedition to Masaccio's chapel in the church of the Carmine, he punched Michelangelo in the face and broke his nose.*

**Carrara marble**
*(below) Michelangelo favoured the marble quarry at Carrara because the stone was so white and pure. He spent months here personally supervising the cutting and shipping of the stone.*

particularly disturbing influence, denouncing the corruption of Florence and prophesying the imminent doom of the sinful city. The invasion of Italy by Charles VIII of France added fuel to the unrest. Apparently, with the words of Savonarola ringing in his ears, Michelangelo packed up and left for Venice in October 1494 – the first of his many 'flights'.

After a period in Venice, Michelangelo went to Bologna, where he remained for a year. He then returned briefly to Florence in 1495 where he carved a life-size figure of a sleeping Cupid. This was such a fine piece of work that one of the Medicis suggested it could be passed off as an antique. According to rumour the Cupid was later sold in Rome behind Michelangelo's back as a classical statue.

## A VISIT TO ROME

In 1496 Michelangelo was summoned to Rome as a result of the famous 'Sleeping Cupid affair' which had made him a reputation. Here, he carved the marble *Bacchus* for the banker, Jacopo Galli, and the famous *Pietà* (p.54), now in St Peter's, for the French Cardinal Jean Bilhères de Lagraulas. The startling beauty and originality of the *Pietà* brought Michelangelo enduring fame. He was soon being heralded as Italy's foremost sculptor. By 1501, he was able to return to Florence as a hero. There he carved the magnificent statue of *David* (p.55) further enhancing his reputation. The statue was placed in front of the Palazzo della

Explorer

**The papal city**
*(above) Michelangelo first visited Rome in 1496, summoned by the cardinal who had bought his statue of Cupid as an antique. It was the first of many long stays in the city, where his patrons included seven popes. Here he accomplished the most remarkable achievement of his career – the painting of the Sistine Chapel ceiling.*

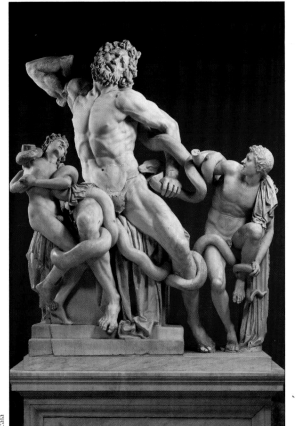

Scala

**The Laocoön**
*(left) Michelangelo was present when this famous antique statue of Apollo's disobedient priest was discovered in Rome in 1506. The twisting poses and violent emotion of the three male figures struggling with the sea serpents had an enormous influence on his art.*

Pio-Clementino Museum, Vatican

# The Tragedy of the Tomb

In 1505, Pope Julius II commissioned Michelangelo to build a monumental tomb to immortalize his memory. This grandiose project plagued Michelangelo for over 40 years. Abandoned by Julius in favour of the rebuilding of St Peter's, the project was revived by successive popes who each modified the design, but then made it impossible for Michelangelo to find the time to complete it. It was finally finished in 1547.

Scala

Raphael/Mass at Bolsena (detail)/Stanza d'Eliodoro, Vatican

Signoria, where it stood as a symbol of Republican freedom, courage and moral virtue.

The legendary sculptor went from strength to strength. Soon after the death of Pope Alexander VI he was summoned back to Rome to serve the new Pope, Julius II. Julius was the first of the seven popes that Michelangelo worked for and their relationship was tempestuous.

In the spring of 1505, Julius commissioned Michelangelo to create a tomb for him. It was to be a free-standing shrine with over 40 statues, a grand monument to himself. The scale of the project suited the scope of Michelangelo's vision, and he spent eight months enthusiastically quarrying marble at Carrara. But the Pope soon began to grow impatient at the lack of results and gradually started to lose interest.

### A PLAN FOR ST PETER'S

By then, the Pope had conceived an even grander plan for the complete rebuilding of the church of St Peter's in Rome, and he had entrusted the design to his favourite architect, Bramante. When Michelangelo returned to Rome, burning with desire to make his magnificent vision live, the Pope refused to see him.

Michelangelo left Rome for Florence in a fury, deliberately leaving the day before the laying of the cornerstone for the new St Peter's. Pope Julius matched his wrath, however, and sent envoys and demands for his return 'by fair means or foul'. Eventually Michelangelo succumbed, and went to

**A Florentine patriot**
*(below) Following the sacking of Rome in 1527, the Florentine republic made Michelangelo their chief of defences. He is shown here directing the building of fortifications, with S. Miniato church in the background.*

Matteo Rosselli/Casa Buonarroti, Florence

the Pope with a rope around his neck – a sarcastic gesture of submission. Julius, who was in a more amenable mood, having just conquered Bologna, rewarded Michelangelo with a commission for a colossal statue of himself, to be cast in bronze. (The statue was later destroyed.)

Michelangelo was still dreaming of completing the tomb, but Julius was bent on redecorating the Sistine ceiling. Michelangelo eventually accepted the commission, possibly goaded on by Bramante's suggestion that he might lack the ability for such a task. But he always insisted that painting was not his trade, and he again tried to get out of the commission when spots of mould started to appear on the first section of his fresco. By 1512, after four years of exhausting labour, however, the ceiling was finally completed. When his work was unveiled, the effect was awe-inspiring and people would travel hundreds of miles to see this work of an 'angel'. As usual, Michelangelo sent the money he received for the work to his demanding family.

Julius died in 1513, leaving money for the completion of his tomb, and Michelangelo moved some marble he had quarried from his workshop near St Peter's to a house in the Macel de' Corvi, which he kept from 1513 until his death. Successive popes were keen that Michelangelo should work for their own glory, and distracted him with other commissions.

**The tomb of Julius II**
*(right) The concept of the tomb changed from a free-standing structure decorated with some 40 figures to a wall tomb in the church of S. Pietro in Vincoli. Finished with the help of another sculptor, only the three lower statues, including the central figure of Moses, are by Michelangelo.*

**Michelangelo's greatest patron**
*(left) During the ten years of his pontificate Julius II commissioned some of Michelangelo's finest works, but they were both strong-willed men, and their relationship was extremely tempestuous. A formidable character, Julius was 'hated by many and feared by all'.*

S. Pietro in Vincoli, Rome

Royal Library, Windsor

Scala

Then, in 1527, Rome was sacked by the Imperial troops of Charles V, a mainly protestant army bent on the destruction of the Papacy. An orgy of murder and pillage followed and Pope Clement VII was imprisoned in the Castel Sant' Angelo. The Medici were yet again expelled from Florence, and the republicans put the artist in charge of the fortifications of his native city. In September 1529, fearing treachery, Michelangelo fled wisely to Venice.

Eventually Pope Clement VII, then restored to power in Rome, wrote to pardon Michelangelo and ordered him to continue work on a chapel for the Medicis at San Lorenzo in Florence. Michelangelo finished the tombs for the Medici chapel, but in 1534, three years after his father's death, he left Florence in the tyrannical grip of Alessandro de' Medici, never to return.

Michelangelo went to Rome, where Pope Clement had in mind a grandiose scheme for the decoration of the altar wall of the Sistine Chapel. Clement died before the painting was begun, but his successor, Paul III, set him to work on the project. *The Last Judgement* (p.61) was painted from 1536 to 1541, and is a terrifying vision expressing the artist's own mental suffering.

### NEW FRIENDS

Michelangelo had always been a practising Catholic and was a deeply pious man. In later life, his religion became profoundly important to him. This was partly the result of his great affection and admiration for Vittoria Colonna, the Marchioness of Pescara – the only woman with whom he had a special relationship.

For Michelangelo was widely believed to be homosexual and it is true that he showed a preoccupation with the male nude unmatched by any other artist. In the 1530s, he seems to have fallen in love with a beautiful young nobleman, Tommaso Cavalieri, to whom he wrote many love sonnets. Michelangelo insisted that their friendship was Platonic – he believed that a beautiful body was the outward manifestation of a beautiful soul.

Michelangelo was naturally a recluse. He was

**The fate of Tityus**
*(above) This drawing was made for Tommaso Cavalieri – a young man for whom Michelangelo developed a passion.*

**The Sistine Chapel**
*(right) On the altar wall is Michelangelo's* Last Judgement, *completed 29 years after the ceiling.*

# A Spiritual Friendship

Michelangelo's first meeting with Vittoria Colonna in 1536 marked the beginning of a unique relationship. A devout woman and poetess who retired from society after the death of her husband 'to serve God more tranquilly', she inspired a deep admiration in Michelangelo and stimulated and intensified his simple religious faith.

# Poem for a Poetess

A man, a god rather, inside a woman,
Through her mouth has his speech,
And this has made me such
I'll never again be mine after I listen.
Ever since she has stolen
Me from myself, I'm sure,
Outside myself I'll give myself my pity.
Her beautiful features summon
Upward from false desire,
So that I see death in all other beauty.
You who bring souls, O lady,
Through fire and water to felicity,
See to it I do not return to me.

(Rime, 235)

Translation by Prof. C. Gilbert

**Sublimated love**
*(left and below) Michelangelo executed several beautiful religious drawings for Vittoria, and exchanged many letters and poems with her. In this famous madrigal, he describes her as a man or god speaking inside a woman. The engraving shows him aged 72, a year before Vittoria's death in 1547.*

melancholic and introverted, but at the same time emotional and explosive. He lived a temperate life, but in a fair degree of domestic squalor which no servant would tolerate for long. He preferred to be alone 'like a genie shut up inside a bottle', contemplating death. In 1544 and 1545 he suffered two illnesses which did actually bring him close to death. Evidently the great papal commissions had weakened his constitution.

Paul III made Michelangelo Architect-in-Chief of St Peter's, and his work on the church continued throughout the rest of his life, under three successive popes – Julius II, Paul IV and Pius IV. He tried to return to the simplicity of his old rival Bramante's design, but St Peter's was not finished in his lifetime, nor exactly to his designs.

Finally, in his old age, Michelangelo also had time to work for himself and the sculptures of this period, such as the *Duomo Pietà* (below), reveal an intense spirituality and tenderness. Pope Julius II used to remark that he would gladly surrender some of his own years and blood to prolong Michelangelo's life, so that the world would not be deprived too soon of the sculptor's genius. He also had a desire to have Michelangelo embalmed so that his remains, like his works, would be eternal. As it happened, Michelangelo outlived Julius II, and was buried with great pomp and circumstance after his death on 18 February 1564.

Scala

### Vittoria Colonna

*(below) One of the outstanding women of the Renaissance, Vittoria Colonna mixed with some of the leading poets and philosophers of the age. She divided her time between a convent in Viterbo, where she devoted herself to poetry and reform within the church, and Rome, where she knew Michelangelo.*

Sebastiano del Piombo/Casa Buonarroti, Florence

Scala

### The Capitol

*(above) The removal of the antique statue of Marcus Aurelius to the Capitol in 1538 prompted Michelangelo to design a new pedestal and draw up plans for the development of the site – one of several architectural schemes for Rome. Although nothing was built in his lifetime, his design was preserved and finally completed in the mid 17th century.*

### The Duomo Pietà

*(right) Michelangelo carved the Pietà when he was in his 70s, intending it for his tomb. Unfinished and smashed because of a flaw in the marble, Michelangelo allowed it to be reassembled by a pupil. The figure of Nicodemus, supporting the body of Christ, is a moving self-portrait of the sculptor.*

Scala

Florence Cathedral

# The Heroic Vision

**Michelangelo displayed his colossal powers of invention and his extravagant technical mastery in the arts of painting, sculpture and architecture, creating a new, inspirational and heroic style.**

During his lifetime and throughout the centuries, Michelangelo's achievement as an artist has been regarded with awe. As Giorgio Vasari wrote:
'. . . the benign ruler of heaven decided to send into the world an artist who would be skilled in each and every craft, whose work alone would teach us how to attain perfection in design (by correct drawing and by the use of contour and light and shadows, so as to obtain relief) and how to use right judgement in sculpture and, in architecture, create buildings which would be comfortable and secure, healthy, pleasant to look at, well-proportioned and richly ornamented.'
For Michelangelo 'was supreme not in one art alone but in all three' – in painting, sculpture and in architecture.

To begin with, Michelangelo displayed his genius through his mastery of the human figure and, in particular, the male nude. Man, according to the Renaissance, was the measure of all things, the centre of the universe. Accordingly, Michelangelo was not interested in creating convincing landscape settings or in the art of portraiture. Only the human figure, treated in an idealized way, was a noble enough vehicle for the expression of his grand conceptions.

Michelangelo's understanding of the human form was influenced by the powerful works of the

Bridgeman Art Library

British Museum, London

**Preliminary studies**
*(left) Michelangelo always made detailed preparatory drawings for his compositions, using boys or men as models. This highly-finished nude is a study for the central figure of his celebrated* Battle of Cascina, *which he only ever completed in 'cartoon' (the working drawing for the mural). Michelangelo chose to show an incident just before the battle, when the Florentine soldiers had stripped off to bathe, only to be startled into action by a cry of alarm.*

Scala

Uffizi, Florence

**The Doni Tondo (1503/4)**
*(left) This Holy Family group shows the hard, sculptural quality of Michelangelo's painting style. The tondo, or circular form, was popular in Florence for depictions of the Madonna and child.*

**Sistine Ceiling fresco**
*(right) The Creation of Sun, Moon and Plants is one of Michelangelo's most original conceptions. The dynamically powerful figure of the Creator is shown in daring foreshortening – a typical display of skill on Michelangelo's part.*

Scala

**The Laurentian Library Staircase**
(*right*) *This extraordinary free-standing staircase was designed by Michelangelo for the Medici's library in Florence.*

**The Awakening Slave**
(*below*) *Michelangelo's four unfinished* Slaves *were originally destined for the Julius Tomb. This figure seems to be struggling to free himself from the stone.*

New Sacristy, San Lorenzo, Florence

**The Medici Tomb sculpture**
(*above*) *Michelangelo created two tombs for the Medici funerary chapel, to Giulio and Lorenzo de' Medici. Lorenzo is shown in a contemplative pose.*

Accademia, Florence

Sistine Chapel, Vatican

painter, Masaccio, and the sculptor, Donatello. But his most vital source of inspiration was the sculpture of antiquity, which he first saw in the garden of Lorenzo de' Medici's palace. The artists of Michelangelo's time were among the first to appreciate the 'liveliness' of classical sculpture. Superior examples, like the *Laocoön* and the *Torso Belvedere*, which had been mentioned by the ancient writer, Pliny the Elder, were in the process of being dug out of the earth. Here were figures who, according to Vasari, 'possessed the appeal and vigour of living flesh', and whose attitudes were natural, graceful and full of movement. One of Michelangelo's earliest works was inspired by a Roman battle sarcophagus, and showed a group of men involved in violent action. These robust, muscular nudes, twisted into a variety of poses, form the basis of Michelangelo's heroic style.

## EMOTIONAL EXPRESSION

In such late works as *The Last Judgement* (pp.60–61), the human body has become a tool for the expression of a whole range of human emotions. The contorted, writhing figures reveal a very personal side to Michelangelo's art: like so many of his works, they are characterized by struggle and, as many commentators have noted, by a sense of agonized frustration. Here, we are presented with a veritable encyclopedia of human movements and gestures, all bearing witness to the awesome power – which his contemporaries called *terribilità* – of Michelangelo's art.

Michelangelo could manipulate the human body as he did because he had a rare understanding of its mechanisms. He put great store by drawing from the model, and throughout his life he dissected corpses – so that he knew the position of every muscle, every sinew, even every tiny blood vessel. Remarkably, he never repeated a gesture, because every detail of his work was imprinted on an incredible visual memory.

The two main areas of his output were fresco painting and sculpting in marble, but for both he relied on preliminary drawings to work out the positioning and articulation of figures and details of anatomy. His drawings show that he thought naturally in three dimensions, as a sculptor would. Light and shade are used emphatically, giving depth to a composition as if it were a relief (a sculpture projecting from a background surface) and suggesting different textures. (In his sculptures Michelangelo liked the contrast of the

## COMPARISONS

# Sculptural Form

In spite of his gigantic achievements as a painter and architect, Michelangelo always regarded his vocation as that of sculptor. Indeed, his greatest works in painting and architecture – the Sistine Ceiling and the rebuilding of St Peter's – were done under protest because they took him away from his beloved marble. He saw painting and drawing in sculptural terms and thought that a picture must be judged in terms of how successfully it conveyed an illusion of being three-dimensional. This attitude is also reflected in works such as *The Taddei Tondo*. Donatello and Masaccio, two of the founding fathers of the Renaissance, were great Florentine predecessors in whom Michelangelo found his ideal of sculptural form fulfilled.

**Donatello (1386-1466)**
**St Mark**
*Donatello was the greatest Italian sculptor before Michelangelo and a major influence on his work. The powerful but relaxed pose of St Mark, with the weight on the right leg, is reflected in Michelangelo's David (p.55).*

**Masaccio (1401-28) detail from The Tribute Money**
*Masaccio died tragically young, but had enormous influence. His mastery of light and perspective gave painting a new sense of solidity and of being three-dimensional. Among Michelangelo's earliest drawings are copies of figures in this majestic fresco.*

Orsanmichele, Florence

Santa Maria del Carmine, Florence

highly polished surface of the skin with the roughness of the hair and parts of the marble which he chose to leave chipped and unfinished.)

Similarly in his paintings, Michelangelo sculpts with his brush, throwing figures into sharp relief by modelling with light and shade. Colour is used simply to fill in the strong outlines. 'I affirm that painting is the better the more it tends towards relief, and relief is the worse the more it tends towards painting' he wrote in a letter, and this attitude is well illustrated by the *Doni Tondo* or Holy Family (p.50) done for his friend, the merchant Angelo Doni (c.1503-4). It is a 'tempera' painting, executed using egg as a medium for the mixing of the paints. The colours are hard and bright and the forms are all sharply in focus.

## TWISTING POSES

The *Doni Tondo* demonstrates how much more interested Michelangelo was in the linear rhythms of a composition and the *contrapposto*, or twisting poses, of his figures, than in the expressive use of colour. He clearly took no sensuous delight in the pigment itself, and he had no time for Leonardo da Vinci's misty *sfumato* technique, although he admired Leonardo's complex grouping of figures.

The same is true of the Sistine Ceiling frescoes (pp.56–9), where the figures look like palely tinted sculptures and the colours of the backgrounds and the drapery are made to harmonize with the tones of the flesh. Michelangelo learnt the process of painting in fresco during his apprenticeship in Ghirlandaio's workshop. At least two layers of plaster – a mixture of slaked lime and sand in water – were applied to the wall or ceiling, and on this the final layer of plaster, or *intonaco*, was laid in sections, according to how much the artist could paint in one day.

The work was completed in sections like this, because the painting was done while the plaster was still wet, so that the water-based colours

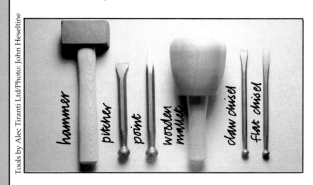

**The sculptor's tools**
*(above) Stonecarvers' tools have changed little through the years. The metal-headed hammer is used with the pitcher and the point to take off large chips of stone and rough out the main forms. Detailed carving is done with a wooden mallet and two kinds of chisel – the claw chisel leaves a furrowed surface, which is smoothed out with the flat chisel. Further surface polish can be obtained with files and abrasive powders.*

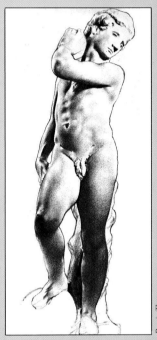

would penetrate deeper. This method, known as *buon fresco*, meant that the surface of the fresco had less tendency to scale and flake and the colours were clearer than if the alternative method of *fresco secco* – painting on dry plaster – was followed.

Buon fresco was thought to be a more difficult and more noble method than fresco secco by the Italian Renaissance painters, because the artist had to paint broadly, quickly and decisively. This suited Michelangelo, who liked to work at great speed and on a grandiose scale.

## FREED FROM THE STONE

Michelangelo always thought of himself as a sculptor, although he certainly did not despise painting. He described sculpting as 'the art of taking away material'. By chipping away the marble, working from the front of the block backwards, he believed that he was liberating an existing image from its imprisoning block. This 'image' was the concept, or *concetto*, that was already in the artist's mind, and to Michelangelo the work was complete when the concetto had been fully realized.

Michelangelo's architecture was also based on sculptural qualities. In his early commissions, such as the San Lorenzo façade and the Medici Tomb chapel, sculpture forms an integral part of the architectural design. Even the Laurentian Library staircase could be conceived of as a sculptural feature; and the later, purely architectural commissions, such as the magnificent dome of St Peter's, reveal a sculptor's attitude towards volume, mass, and the surface play of light and shade. He disrupted the harmony and stability of early Renaissance designs, and just as he was not afraid to distort human anatomy in the interest of conveying emotion, so he used architectural elements in an expressive and unorthodox way.

*THE ARTIST AT WORK continues on page 64.*

The word contrapposto originally described a pose in which a figure's weight is borne mainly by one leg, giving a feeling of muscular tension and relaxation. Later it was applied to the kind of twisting poses at which Michelangelo so obviously excelled.

Réunion des Musées Nationaux

Louvre, Paris

**A master of anatomy**
*(above and right) Throughout Michelangelo's long career, the heroic male nude was the dominant subject of his painting and sculpture: he thought of his figures as imitating the work of God. Like Leonardo, Michelangelo was a consummate master of anatomy and wrote 'who is so barbarous as not to understand that the foot of a man is nobler than his shoe, and his skin nobler than that of the sheep with which he is clothed?'*

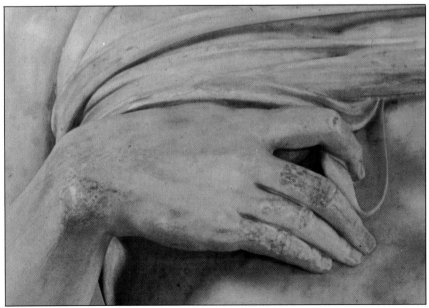

# Gallery

Having trained as a painter and a sculptor, Michelangelo left Florence and travelled to the holy city of Rome. Here, he sculpted a pietà. The delicacy and technical brilliance of the work made his reputation, and on his return to Florence he was entrusted with a major commission – the famous David.

The grace and elegance of the Pietà and

**Pietà** *1497-1500*
height: 5'8½"
St Peter's, Rome

*Michelangelo carved the exquisite St Peter's Pietà for a French cardinal in Rome. His contemporaries were immediately impressed by the exceptional beauty of the work – in which every fold of drapery was finely sculpted and polished. A few complained, however, about the comparatively youthful appearance of the Virgin.*

Scala

*Michelangelo Buonarroti*

the heroic grandeur of David are combined in the Sistine Ceiling frescoes which demonstrate the full scope of Michelangelo's genius. Over 20 years later, he returned to the Sistine Chapel to paint the terrifying Last Judgement. In this austere masterpiece the gentle linear rhythms of the Pietà are replaced by a fuller, more expressive style.

**David** *1501-4*
height: 13'5¼" Accademia, Florence

*In 1501, Michelangelo returned to Florence to undertake one of his most important official commissions. On his arrival, he was given an enormous block of marble, which had been lying abandoned in the cathedral office of works. Some 40 years earlier, another sculptor had begun to carve a figure from it, but had bungled the attempt. Now the City of Florence wanted Michelangelo to produce a monumental figure of David, which would symbolize the Republican virtues of courage and fortitude. The block was tall, very shallow and considerably flawed. Nevertheless, Michelangelo boldly surmounted these obstacles, sculpting the figure in incredible anatomical detail. He chose to show David just before his battle with Goliath: the young biblical hero stands, with his sling over his shoulder, frozen in a pose of tense anticipation and defiance.*

Scala

**The Sistine Ceiling** *1508-12*
**Detail: The Delphic Sibyl** *1509*
Vatican, Rome

*As part of the Sistine ceiling decoration, Michelangelo painted five pagan Sibyls – ancient Seers who prophesied the coming of Christ. The Delphic Sibyl was the first to be completed: a lovely sculptural figure seated on an architectural throne.*

**The Sistine Ceiling** *1508-12*
**Detail: The Libyan Sibyl** *1511*
Vatican, Rome

*The Libyan Sibyl was painted two years after the Delphic Sibyl and
shows the extent to which Michelangelo's confidence had grown. The
figure, twisted into an elaborate pose, is so large that Michelangelo had
to lower the platform for her feet.*

Scala

**The Sistine Ceiling** *1508-12*
**Detail: The Creation of Adam** *1511*
Vatican, Rome

*On the vault of the Sistine Ceiling, Michelangelo painted nine scenes*
*from Genesis, of which the most famous is* The Creation of Adam.
*Here, the listless body of Adam is about to be animated by the spirit of*
*God at the gentle touch of their fingertips. This potent image may*
*have been suggested by the Latin hymn* Veni Creator Spiritus, *in*
*which God restores strength and courage to the weakened flesh with*
*a touch of his finger.*

**The Last Judgement** 1536-41
45' × 40' Sistine Chapel, Vatican Rome

*The gigantic fresco of The Last Judgement was commissioned by Pope Paul III to adorn the altar wall of the Sistine Chapel. Michelangelo decided to paint it alone, without the help of assistants; he even refused the aid of physicians after he had suffered a heavy fall from the scaffolding. The awesome scheme was largely inspired by the words of the Latin hymn, Dies Irae, and by Dante's Inferno which Michelangelo knew off by heart. As soon as the fresco was unveiled, controversy raged about the nudity of the figures, which was considered unsuitable, not to say obscene, in its religious context. Eventually, it was decided to give all the figures loin-cloths or drapery and the task was undertaken soon after Michelangelo's death by a small team of artists, contemptuously nicknamed 'the breeches-makers'.*

**Detail from The Last Judgement: Christ the Judge**

*In the centre of the fresco, Michelangelo depicted the athletic figure of Christ, surrounded by an aura of light.*
*St Bartholomew sits on a cloud at his feet, holding a flayed skin on which the artist has painted a tragic self-portrait.*

**Detail from The Last Judgement: A Condemned Soul**

*In the lower portion of the fresco, Michelangelo painted the figures of the Damned being dragged down to Hell.*
*One soul has abandoned all hope: in the midst of scenes of titanic struggle, he covers his face in sheer terror and despair.*

## THE MAKING OF A MASTERPIECE

# The Sistine Ceiling

On 10 May 1508 Michelangelo signed the contract for the decoration of the Sistine Ceiling – a momentous task which was to pose one of the greatest human as well as artistic challenges. The work had been commissioned by Pope Julius II, whose uncle, Sixtus IV, had authorized the building of the Sistine Chapel in the Vatican. On the walls were 15th-century frescoes showing scenes from the life of Moses and Christ, while the ceiling was a traditional star-spangled blue. Julius, however, who was bent on the whole-scale 'restoration' of Christian Rome, wanted something grander and more 'progressive'.

By July, the scaffolding was in place and the cardinals, who had complained of the noise and rubble, were able to conduct their services in peace. A few weeks later, five young assistants arrived in Rome, but on finding the door of the Chapel bolted, they took the hint and returned to Florence. In the end, Michelangelo painted the ceiling almost entirely alone, triumphing over months of tremendous physical discomfort.

The completed ceiling was unveiled on 31 October 1512. 'When the work was thrown open', reported Giorgio Vasari, 'the whole world came running to see what Michelangelo had done; and certainly it was such as to make everyone speechless with astonishment.'

Scala

Scala

**Athletic 'ignudi'**
(left) The 'ignudi', or nudes, seated directly above the Prophets and Sibyls, may represent 'angels', although they seem to be an entirely personal contribution. They support bronze medallions, attached to garlands or acorns – the heraldic device of the Della Rovere family of Julius II.

**Christian parallels**
(right) The prophet Jonah is given pride of place over the altar because he prefigures the Resurrection of Christ: just as he emerged from the belly of a fish, so Christ emerged from the tomb. Michelangelo was particularly pleased with the figure's dramatically fore-shortened pose.

Scala

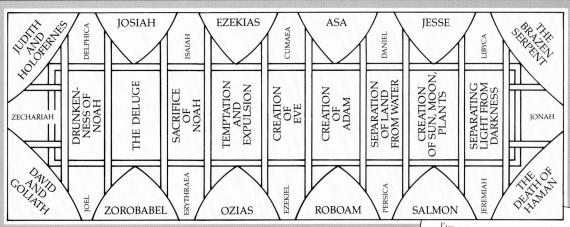

| | | | | | | | | |
|---|---|---|---|---|---|---|---|---|
| JUDITH AND HOLOFERNES | JOSIAH | EZEKIAS | ASA | JESSE | THE BRAZEN SERPENT |
| | DELPHICA | ISAIAH | CUMAEA | DANIEL | LIBYCA | |
| ZECHARIAH | DRUNKEN-NESS OF NOAH | THE DELUGE | SACRIFICE OF NOAH | TEMPTATION AND EXPULSION | CREATION OF EVE | CREATION OF ADAM | SEPARATION OF LAND FROM WATER | CREATION OF SUN, MOON, PLANTS | SEPARATING LIGHT FROM DARKNESS | JONAH |
| DAVID AND GOLIATH | JOEL | ERYTHRAEA | EZEKIEL | PERSICA | JEREMIAH | THE DEATH OF HAMAN |
| | ZOROBABEL | OZIAS | ROBOAM | SALMON | |

## The grandiose scheme

*(left and above) According to Michelangelo, the pope let him devise his own scheme for the ceiling, although he clearly had theological advice. Pagan Sibyls and Hebrew Prophets, who foresaw the Christian era, are interspersed with lunettes and spandrels of the Ancestors of Christ. The four corner spandrels show Old Testament heroes, while the nine scenes on the vault illustrate the story of Noah and the Creation.*

## A feat of endurance

*(below) Michelangelo painted the ceiling standing (not lying down) on the scaffolding, reaching overhead with his brush. In a comic verse (right) to his friend, Giovanni da Pistoia, he complained that he was 'bending like a Syrian bow'. According to Vasari, his sight was so badly impaired, that he couldn't read or look at drawings 'save with his head turned backwards', for months afterwards.*

I've got myself a goiter from this strain,
As water gives the cats in Lombardy
Or maybe it is in some other country;
My belly's pushed by force beneath my chin.

My beard toward Heaven, I feel the back of my brain
Upon my neck, I grow the breast of a Harpy;
My brush, above my face continually,
Makes it a splendid floor by dripping down.

My loins have penetrated to my paunch,
My rump's a crupper, as a counterweight,
And pointless the unseeing steps I go.

In front of me my skin is being stretched
While it folds up behind and forms a knot,
And I am bending like a Syrian bow.

And judgment, hence must grow,
Borne in mind, peculiar and untrue;
You cannot shoot well when the gun's askew.

John, come to the rescue
Of my dead painting now, and of my honour;
I'm not in a good place, and I'm no painter.

Translation by Prof. C. Gilbert

Michael McGuinness

**The Fall of Man**
(*right*) *In this panel, Michelangelo combined the two scenes of the Temptation and Expulsion from Paradise. The power and grandeur of the figures of Adam and Eve reveal his debt to the painter Masaccio.*

**Red chalk studies**
(*below*) *This sheet of drawings for the Libyan Sibyl (p.57) shows that Michelangelo used a male rather than a female model – a normal practice in those times. The model is drawn in an elegant, highly artificial pose.*

Metropolitan Museum of Art, New York

# Fresco Cartoons

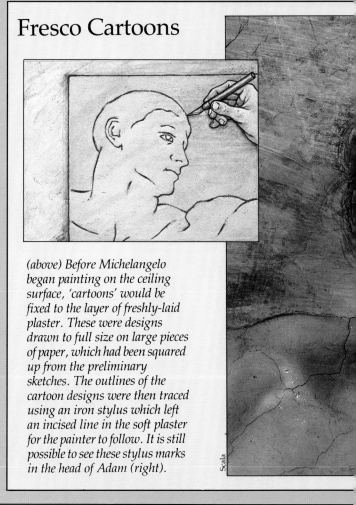

(*above*) *Before Michelangelo began painting on the ceiling surface, 'cartoons' would be fixed to the layer of freshly-laid plaster. These were designs drawn to full size on large pieces of paper, which had been squared up from the preliminary sketches. The outlines of the cartoon designs were then traced using an iron stylus which left an incised line in the soft plaster for the painter to follow. It is still possible to see these stylus marks in the head of Adam (right).*

Scala

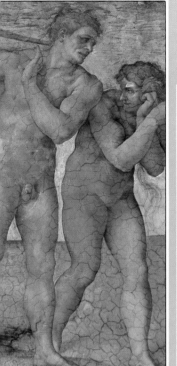

> 'Every detail reflects Michelangelo's genius; and every single feature is manifestly inspired and beyond praise.'   Vasari

Photos: Vatican Museums

### Before and after cleaning

*(above) In the 1980s, restoration work began on the Sistine Ceiling frescoes. Centuries of grime was removed to reveal the original state of Michelangelo's paintings. This lunette with Matthan, one of the Ancestors of Christ, shows that the artist's colours are much crisper and brighter than is often supposed.*

### Classical inspiration

*(right) Many of the figures on the ceiling, particularly the muscular 'ignudi', are ideal reconstructions of the famous* Belvedere Torso. *This marble sculpture, signed by Apollonius, was one of the jewels of Julius II's collection. Michelangelo described it as 'the work of a man who knew more than nature'.*

Scala

Pio-Clementino Museum, Vatican

# New St Peter's

**Over 1000 years after the Emperor Constantine built a church at the site of St Peter's grave, it became the dream of Renaissance popes to rebuild the holy shrine – for the glory of God and of Rome.**

St Peter's in Rome is hallowed by a tradition that no other church can match. For almost from the moment that Christ's martyred disciple St Peter – whom Catholics regard as the first pope – was buried there, a shrine has stood at the site of his grave.

Constantine the Great, the emperor who adopted Christianity as the official religion of Rome, consecrated a basilica over St Peter's grave on 18 November 326. The building was huge by any standards (well over 100 yards long), and by the middle of the 15th century it was in danger of collapse. Pope Nicholas V resolved to rebuild it but when he died in 1455, little work had been done.

Half a century later, Pope Julius II decided to build a completely new church. To contemplate pulling down Constantine's venerable building, which had stood for more than 1000 years, took astonishing self-confidence, but Julius – the greatest artistic patron of the day – was not a man to do things by halves. He intended that the church should, in Vasari's words, 'surpass in beauty, invention, order, size, richness and decoration all the buildings ever erected there'.

## THE SALE OF INDULGENCES

Financing so gigantic a building project was a major problem. Even before the foundation stone was laid, Julius had appealed for funds to monarchs, nobles and bishops throughout Europe, and later he encouraged the selling of 'indulgences' to swell the coffers. An indulgence was a remission of the punishment due for sin and although in theory they could be given only to those who had truly repented, in practice sinners could 'buy' a reduction of the time they would spend in purgatory after death.

This abuse of papal power was one of the sparks that ignited the Protestant Reformation, and it is ironic that the building of a shrine to the first pope should indirectly lead to an attack on the authority of his successors.

Julius entrusted the design of the building to Donato Bramante, the most celebrated architect of the High Renaissance, whose buildings revived

**Bramante's Tempietto**
*(right) This little circular chapel was built on the supposed site of St Peter's death. In its symmetry and proportions, it is perhaps the perfect Renaissance building, and the basis for Bramante's design for St Peter's.*

Mauro Pucciarelli

Scala

**Old St Peter's (326 AD)**
*(left) Constantine's basilica was vast in size, but simple in structure. This interior view shows the long nave, double aisles, and plain timber roof. The church was in a state of serious disrepair by the 15th century, when Pope Nicholas V decided to rebuild it. At the beginning of the 16th century, Bramante knocked down a great deal of the old church, but certain elements remained intact until the 17th century.*

the grandeur of ancient Rome. The foundation stone of new St Peter's was laid by Julius himself on 18 April 1506 and a splendid medal was struck to commemorate the occasion.

Bramante was over 60 at this time, so he was determined to press on with all possible speed. He employed a team of 2,500 men on the demolition work, and there was such wholesale destruction of fittings and furnishings from the old basilica that Bramante was nicknamed 'Il Ruinante'.

The most striking feature of Bramante's design was the vast central dome: he set the scale for the building with the four massive piers he built to support it. The piers and the arches joining them were completed by the time Bramante died in

**New St Peter's**
*(right) Over 150 years after Bramante started work on the new St Peter's, the great sculptor Bernini began the construction of the curved colonnade which sweeps up towards the church and its majestic dome. The arms of the colonnade enclose the vast piazza in which massive crowds gather to receive the Pope's blessing.*

### The Emperor and the Pope

(left) This 17th century engraving shows an imaginary meeting between the early Christian emperor, Constantine, and the Renaissance pope, Julius II. The Pope is showing the Emperor his plan for the new St Peter's superimposed on Constantine's original church. The first of the Renaissance popes to devote time, effort and money to the rebuilding, Julius saw himself as a prince as well as a pope. The year in which the foundation medal for the new church was struck, he successfully led his papal army in a war against Bologna.

### The foundation medal

(below) Struck in 1506, this medal shows Bramante's design for St Peter's. Its huge central dome was to be surrounded by four smaller ones set above the arms of a Greek cross, with a fifth dome set over the portico.

Fotomas Index

1514, and although the succeeding architects produced designs that varied a great deal in appearance, they were all committed to the idea of Bramante's great dome.

Julius had died the year before Bramante and, with the departure of the two principal protagonists, the building works lost momentum. Julius' successor, Leo X, appointed a team of three men to take over from Bramante: Raphael, Fra Giocondo and Giuliano da Sangallo. The latter two died in 1515 and 1516 respectively, leaving Raphael in sole command.

## RAPHAEL'S PLAN

Raphael soon prepared a new plan for St Peter's. Bramante's design was a 'Greek' cross, one in which the four 'arms' (nave, chancel and transepts) which centred on the dome were of equal length. But Raphael proposed a 'Latin' cross, in which one arm (the nave) was longer than the other three. A Latin cross was convenient for extravagant processions, but the symmetry of a Greek cross was thought to symbolize the perfection of God. After Raphael's death in 1520, his successor, Baldassare Peruzzi, reverted to a Greek cross plan.

The building work was brought to a violent and abrupt halt in 1527, when the holy city was invaded by the massed troops of Charles V, the Holy Roman Emperor. After the devastation of the Sack of Rome, St Peter's remained in a ruinous state until the 1530s, when a new pope, Paul III, supplied some much-needed momentum. In his previous role as Cardinal Alessandro Farnese,

Dan Budnik/The John Hillelson Agency

Paul had commissioned building the Palazzo Farnese, the grandest palace of the period. And he appointed the designer of the palace, Antonio da Sangallo the Younger, as architect to St Peter's.

Paul III was so keen to press on with the church that he revived the selling of indulgences and even diverted to the building fund some money that had been collected for a crusade against the Turks. Sangallo repaired the structural damage caused by neglect, and designed a spectacular wooden model to show his own plans for the building. The model is undoubtedly a superb work of carpentry, but the design is marked by fussiness rather than grandeur.

## MICHELANGELO'S TRANSFORMATION

When Sangallo died in 1546, Michelangelo reluctantly became his successor (the pope had to force him to take the job). Michelangelo complained that architecture was not his vocation, and according to Vasari, he embarked on the enterprise 'to his immense dismay and completely against his will'. However, he soon found his customary strength of purpose. He refused payment, saying he was doing the work for 'the love of God and in honour of St Peter', and insisted on complete control and absolute freedom of action. He pulled down part of Sangallo's work and, in Vasari's words, 'diminished the size of St Peter's but increased its grandeur'. He reverted to Bramante's centrally-planned design and replaced Sangallo's fussiness with monumental simplicity.

Paul III died in 1549 but his successors gave Michelangelo their support, and by the time he himself died in 1564, the building had been transformed. The circular drum of the dome was virtually complete and the outer walls were well advanced. In general, his immediate successors

Passignano/Michelangelo presenting the model of St Peter's to Paul IV/Casa Buonarroti, Florence

continued his design faithfully, although the great dome – completed by Giacomo della Porta in 1590 – is steeper in outline than that of Michelangelo's wooden model. Della Porta's assistant was the brilliant engineer Domenico Fontana, and it may be that the change in shape was needed to increase structural stability.

## LATIN CROSS RESTORED

Another change to Michelangelo's design was made in 1605, when Pope Paul V decided to lengthen the nave and recreate a Latin cross plan. He entrusted the work to Carlo Maderno, who demolished the parts of the old basilica that still stood, overcame problems caused by an underground stream, and marshalled his huge workforce with such skill that the façade was

M. van Heemskerck/Gabinetto Disegni, Florence

**A ruinous state**
(left) Between Bramante's death in 1514 and Sangallo's work in the 1530s, the rebuilding programme lost its impetus. In this contemporary drawing, St Peter's looks like an ancient ruin, with weeds growing in its crevices.

**Michelangelo's design**
*(left) Michelangelo was an old man of 72 when Pope Paul III ordered him to take on the St Peter's project. Rejecting Sangallo's plan (below), Michelangelo revived the monumental simplicity of Bramante's original design. This painting shows him presenting his model to his last papal patron, Paul IV.*

completed in 1612, and the nave in 1616. On 18 November 1626, Pope Urban VIII consecrated the church, exactly 1,300 years after the consecration of Constantine's original basilica.

## BERNINI'S INTERIOR DECORATION

Urban VIII was the great patron of the artist who concludes the St Peter's story: Gianlorenzo Bernini, a genius almost as titanic as Michelangelo. Bernini, who like Michelangelo regarded himself as primarily a sculptor, supervised much of the lavish interior decoration of St Peter's which is, without doubt, in a much more ornate and

dramatic style than Michelangelo would have envisaged. This work included making and erecting the immense bronze Baldacchino or altar canopy over the site of St Peter's grave, and in 1656 beginning the massive colonnade that encloses the piazza in front of St Peter's, reaching out to embrace the pilgrims who gather for the Pope's blessing.

But it is Bernini's sweeping colonnade and Michelangelo's soaring dome, that are the parts of the new St Peter's that stay longest in the memory of visitors to Rome, and which are two of the most impressive and influential designs in the history of architecture.

**An elaborate model**
*(left) Sangallo's large-scale wooden model of St Peter's took seven years to build. To Bramante's original Greek cross plan, he added an elaborate vestibule flanked by two massive towers.*

**The great dome**
*(right) When Michelangelo died in 1564, the dome was built up to the drum. It was completed by Giacomo della Porta, who gave it a slightly steeper outline. The stone ribs, which sweep up from the drum to the lantern, add to the impression of vitality.*

Mauro Pucciarelli

**A lavish interior**
*(right) Over 40 years after Michelangelo's death, Pope Paul V recommenced the destruction of what was left of Constantine's church, employing Carlo Maderno as Architect in Chief. Maderno elongated the nave, so that the church became a Latin cross once more. And a generation later, Pope Urban VIII commissioned Bernini to make the huge and elaborate bronze Baldacchino over the supposed exact spot of St Peter's grave. Bernini also supervised the lavishly ornate decorations of the interior.*

Scala

# A Year in the Life 1527

While Michelangelo worked in Florence, Rome was ransacked by German troops. Pope Clement VII was held prisoner and was soon to face another crisis – Henry VIII, desperate for a male heir, wanted a divorce, and if the Pope refused, the dominion of the Catholic Church in England was at risk.

By the beginning of the year, King Francis I of France and Charles V, Holy Roman Emperor, had been waging war, on and off, for five years, with Italy as the principal battleground. Charles had had to divert many of his resources to meet renewed Turkish aggression in central Europe, and was hard pressed, both financially and militarily. His troops in Italy, many of them German mercenaries, were ill-fed and ill-clad. Their pay was in arrears, and mutiny broke out, as the troops resolved to pay themselves with the plunder of enemy cities.

## A CITY IN RUINS

The soldiers' first aim was Florence, but finding it protected by a Venetian army, they turned their sights on Rome. On the

**A building boom in Spain**
(left) Charles V's palace at Granada was begun in 1527 to the designs of the architect Pedro Machuca. This was a time of a great flowering of building in Spain, partly inspired by the flow of gold and silver from the Americas.

**Landfall in Hawaii**
(above) A group of shipwrecked Spanish sailors landed in the Hawaiian Islands in 1527 and settled there. The islands were rediscovered in 1778 by Captain Cook, who was murdered there by natives in 1779.

**Pizzaro in Peru**
(right) The Spanish adventurer Francisco Pizzaro explored Peru from 1524 to 1527. He returned four years later, conquering the Inca Empire and founding the city of Lima in 1535. He was assassinated in 1541.

72

misty morning of 6 May, they breached the western walls and took the defenceless city by storm. The Eternal City had fallen to invaders many times before, but never had it suffered a worse fate than now. 'Hell itself was a more beautiful sight to behold', remarked one onlooker.

The Lutheran troops found in their faith a justification for vicious attacks on churches, monasteries and the clergy – had not Luther himself long predicted the destruction of Rome? Forty thousand soldiers murdered, tortured, raped, looted and destroyed for four terrible days, during which 4,000 people died and two-thirds of the city was left in ruins. Hardly a house was left untouched and the Vatican was almost gutted. The longer the occupation went on, the worse the damage got, and in the months that followed surviving houses were ransacked.

Pope Clement VII was prisoner in the Castel Sant' Angelo, where he had fled at the first sign of impending disaster. Negotiations with his captors failed and he remained prisoner until December, when he managed to escape to Orvieto, perhaps with the connivance of his guards, who were far from happy at guarding a prisoner who could endanger their souls.

## EXPULSION OF THE MEDICI

The Sack of Rome was followed by a debilitating loss of morale as fear and bankruptcy took over. Florence, long sickened by the autocratic rule of the Medici, took this cue to expel them and declare a republic in their place. Michelangelo, whose work on the Medici Chapel and the Laurentian Library

**The Sack of Rome**
*(right) The brutal pillaging of Rome by troops of the Emperor Charles V was one of the blackest events in the history of the city. Pope Clement VII fled from the Vatican (centre) and was held prisoner in the Castel Sant' Angelo (the large circular building on the right).*

Image Bank/Bullaty/Lomeo

Mauro Pucciarelli

**The Turkish conqueror**
*(left) In 1527 Suleiman the Magnificent, Sultan of the Ottoman Empire, was pursuing his conquests in Europe. He had defeated the Hungarians at Mohács in the previous year, and now added large parts of their country to his vast territories.*

**A father of modern medicine**
*(right) The Swiss physician, Paracelsus, began teaching at the University of Basel in 1527 and in the following year published the first manual of surgery. Although much of his work was rooted in superstition, he established the importance of chemistry in medicine.*

Topkapi/Istanbul

Mauro Pucciarelli

Rubens/Paracelsus/Musée des Beaux Arts, Brussels

was brusquely interrupted by the Florentine uprising, threw himself into the politics of his city, taking charge of the construction of fortifications.

## THE NEW RELIGION

There was upheaval in the rest of Europe too – not solely political, but also religious. Luther's Reformation, under way in Germany for a decade now, continued to gain ground, with the founding of the first Protestant University at Marburg in 1527. The new religion spread to Scandinavia, where the monarchs, like the German princes, saw in Lutheranism the chance to enrich themselves at the expense of the Church and to control religion in their countries.

The seeds of the Reformation were also sown in England in 1527, with Henry VIII's petition to Pope Clement to annul his marriage to Catherine of Aragon, who had failed to produce a male heir. In other circumstances, the Pope would no doubt have obliged, but Catherine was Charles V's aunt and Charles V was in control of Rome and the papacy. If Clement agreed, he would incur Charles' wrath; if, on the other hand, he refused, England might defect from Rome – for this was the threat put to him by Henry's chief minister, Cardinal Wolsey. In the face of Clement's understandable evasiveness, Henry (who only a few years earlier had received the title 'defender of the faith' for his support of the papacy against Luther) severed England from the Church of Rome, divorced Catherine and in 1533 married Anne Boleyn.

Lauros-Giraudon

Musée Condé/Chantilly

Mary Evans Picture Library

Scala

SANCTISSIMO. IN. CHRIS

**A queen in waiting**
(above left) Anne Boleyn was appointed lady-in-waiting to Catherine of Aragon in 1527. The king secretly married Anne in 1533, a few months before his divorce from Catherine was official. Anne was accused of adultery and executed in 1536.

**Death of Machiavelli**
(left) The Florentine political theorist Niccolò Machiavelli died in his native city in 1527. His reputation rests mainly on his book The Prince, in which he argues that statecraft should be based on expediency, not morality.

**The king's divorce**
(above) In 1527 Henry VIII petitioned Pope Clement VII to allow him to divorce Catherine of Aragon. Years of procrastination followed, and eventually Henry severed England's connections with the Church of Rome.

Raphael/Self-Portrait/Uffizi, Florence

# ·RAPHAEL·VRBINAS·

## 1483-1520

Raffaello Sanzio – Raphael – was the perfect Renaissance artist. Gracious and charming as a man, and a painter of superlative skill, he seemed to be the living embodiment of the Renaissance ideal. Though neither as innovative as Leonardo nor as sculptural as Michelangelo, he painted with a beauty of line and colour, and a harmony in composition, that surpassed them both.

Raphael is closely associated with his birthplace, Urbino, but he painted most of his great works – the lovely Madonnas and breathtaking frescoes – in Florence and Rome. In these cities, he was showered with commissions and was one of the greatest painters of his age. But illness struck him down at the height of his fame; he died of fever on 6 April 1520, his 37th birthday.

# The Princely Painter

**Raphael's outstanding talent was matched by his graceful manner.
His courteous nature and constant entourage led Vasari to comment
that he lived 'more like a prince than a painter'.**

## Key Dates

**1483** born in Urbino in central Italy

**1494** orphaned and made a ward of his uncle

**1500** works in Perugino's workshop in Perugia

**1504** moves to Florence

**1508** receives commission from Pope Julius II to paint the first *Stanza*

**1511** first major project for Agostino Chigi

**1514** paints *Madonna della Sedia*

**1515** appointed as Conservator of Roman Antiquities in Rome

**1517** paints *Transfiguration*

**1520** dies at the age of 37

Raffaello Sanzio – Raphael – was born on 6 April 1483, in the central Italian city of Urbino. Little is known of his mother, Magia Ciarla, but his father Giovanni was a poet and painter who worked intermittently at the elegant Court of Urbino. The Ducal Court had been a major centre of artistic activity since the middle of the 15th century and these early connections proved important to Raphael, who enjoyed the friendship and patronage of the Court throughout his short life.

### THE YOUNG ORPHAN

By nature Raphael was gentle and modest, and his boyhood familiarity with Court ways no doubt helped to foster the cultured demeanour which endeared him to a series of influential patrons. The young Raphael must also have watched his father at work on his various commissions, and although Giovanni's talent was relatively modest, the atmosphere of artistic activity stimulated the boy's own desire to paint.

In 1491, Raphael's mother died. By 1494 Giovanni too was dead, leaving Raphael an orphan at the age of 11. He was made a ward of his paternal uncle, a priest named Bartolomeo, although he seems to have remained closer to his maternal uncle Simone, with whom he

Ashmolean Museum, Oxford

**The ideal city**
*(left) On a hill above the olive groves of the Marches, Raphael's birthplace of Urbino was seen as an ideal Renaissance city – a focus of learning and all the arts.*

**The young Raphael?**
*(above) This picture of a young man is probably by Raphael and may well be a self-portrait painted around 1506, soon after he arrived in Florence at the age of 21.*

Susan Griggs Agency

corresponded for the rest of his life.

We know almost nothing of Raphael's activities during the following six years, but by May 1500 he had left Urbino and was almost certainly in Perugia, in the workshop of Pietro Perugino. Perugino's works have often been underrated in modern times, but in the late 15th century he was one of Italy's foremost painters. When Raphael arrived in Perugia, Perugino was working on a series of frescoes for the Collegio del Cambio (the Bankers' Guild Hall), and Raphael may well have assisted him. From the beginning of his stay with Perugino, however, Raphael was working independently, or with his compatriot Evangelista di Piandimeleto, and is described as 'magister' or

## The flowering of Florence
*(left) When Raphael arrived in Florence in 1504, the Renaissance culture of the city was at its peak with elegant courtiers and eminent artists thronging the streets.*

'master' in the contracts he received.

Raphael stayed with Perugino for four years or so, painting altarpieces and banners for churches in Perugia, and for the neighbouring town of Città di Castello. He also maintained his links with the Court of Urbino, painting several exquisite panels of saints for the crippled and impotent Duke, Guidobaldo da Montefeltro (p.82).

Soon, however, his thoughts turned further afield. From the very beginning, Raphael's career was marked by an avid desire to learn, and to assimilate new ideas. He probably realized that Perugino had taught him all he could, and decided to move to Florence, arriving there in the autumn of 1504 at the age of 21. The experience of Florence must have been truly exhilarating for the young artist, for these were times of great excitement in the Tuscan capital. Michelangelo's marble *David* had just been installed in front of the Town Hall, and Leonardo was at work on the *Battle of Anghiari* for the Great Council Chamber.

### IN FLORENCE AND ROME

Raphael responded eagerly to the challenge of his new environment. Fired by his experience of Leonardo's drawings, he began to experiment with the theme of the Virgin and Child, producing the first of the beautiful Madonnas for which he is best known. These Madonnas, together with the occasional portrait, provided the bulk of his commissions during his Florentine years.

In 1508 Raphael received a commission which was to change the course of his career – the

Francesco Ubertini/Street Scene in Florence/Rijksmuseum, Amsterdam

## Raphael's mentor
*(below) Raphael's years with Perugino in Perugia clearly left a mark – this painting by Perugino shows the same grace and harmony of composition.*

## Homely fresco
*(right) In the house where Raphael was born in Urbino, there is a fresco which may have been painted by his father – or may be Raphael's earliest work.*

Scala

Perugino/Donation of the Keys/Sistine Chapel, Rome

Casa Santi, Urbino/Scala

decoration of the Papal Apartments, or 'Stanze', for Julius II. In 1507, Julius, in a characteristic outburst of rage, decided that he could no longer live in the Borgia Apartments, surrounded by the flagrantly self-advertising frescoes commissioned by his hated predecessor, Alexander VI. Accordingly, in 1508 he enlisted a team of artists to decorate four rooms on the second floor of the Vatican Palace. The team included the Milanese artist Bramantino, the Sienese 'Il Sodoma', and Raphael's own master Perugino. Work was already in progress when the young Raphael was summoned to the Papal Court in Rome and given full responsibility for the decorations. This included the right to paint over the work that had already been carried out, although with characteristic diplomacy Raphael left intact the ceiling paintings begun by Perugino.

It remains something of a mystery why

**The Judgement of Paris**
*(left) Prints like this, made by the engraver Marcantonio Raimondi from Raphael's designs, introduced Raphael's works to an unprecedented number of people.*

Giraudon

# The Courtier

Under the guiding hand of the Duchess, Elisabetta Gonzaga, the Ducal Court of Urbino in the early 16th century cultivated the ideal of the perfect courtier – combining elegance in dress and manners with prowess in sport and the arts and great learning. Baldassare Castiglione (1478-1529) celebrated these qualities in his enormously influential book *The Courtier*, a series of imaginary dialogues published in 1528. Raphael was in many ways the ideal courtier – graceful, charming and highly accomplished in artistic, intellectual and physical pursuits. Raphael's works, with their poise and balance, seem to embody the same courtly ideals.

Louvre, Paris

**Baldassare Castiglione**
*(left and above) In this portrait, Raphael paints his friend, the author of* The Courtier *(title page below), in the image of the ideal courtier – soberly and elegantly dressed, and in a relaxed and easy pose.*

Lauros-Giraudon

**Knight choosing between Virtue and Pleasure**
*(left) This allegorical painting displays Raphael's espousal with courtly ideals.*

Raphael/An Allegory/National Gallery, London

IL LIBRO
DEL
CORTEGIANO
DEL CONTE
BALDASSAR CASTIGLIONE

EDIZIONE FORMATA SOPRA QUELLA D'ALDO, 1528, RISCONTRATA CON ALTRE DELLE PIU' RIPUTATE, ED ARRICCHITA DI UN COPIOSO INDICE DELLE MATERIE.

MILANO
PER GIOVANNI SILVESTRI
M. DCCC. XXII.

Raphael/Pope Julius II/National Gallery, London

Réunion des Musées Nationaux

## Holy patron

*(left) Pope Julius II was one of Raphael's greatest patrons, and the frescoes Raphael painted for Julius in the Papal Apartments – including the famous School of Athens – are among the most breathtaking creations of the Renaissance.*

## Raphael in Rome

*(below) This fanciful 19th-century painting sums up the legendary days when Raphael (in the centre), Leonardo (on the steps) and Michelangelo (shown in the foreground) were all working in Rome; note the 'Madonna and Child'.*

discreetly installed to catch the precious objects which were then retrieved at the end of the day.

To further enrich his villa, Chigi asked Raphael to paint a fresco in the garden loggia, showing the *Triumph of Galatea*, loosely based on a scene from classical literature. The success of this fresco led to a series of further commissions from Chigi, including the design of his funerary chapel in the church of Santa Maria del Popolo, and the decoration of a second loggia at his villa (p.81).

By the middle of 1511 Raphael had begun work on the second of the apartments for Julius II, the Stanza d'Eliodoro – 'the room of Heliodorus' (p.99). Julius did not live to see the room completed, for he died in February 1513, but the loss of this remarkable patron made little difference to Raphael's career, for the new Pope, Leo X, swiftly recognized his talent. The Stanza d'Eliodoro was completed under Leo's auspices, and he rapidly engaged Raphael in a wealth of new and lucrative projects.

The year 1514 saw Raphael at the height of his career. In August he was formally appointed Papal Architect, in succession to his friend and fellow-

Raphael, with little experience of working in fresco, and no large-scale works to his name, was entrusted with such a momentous task. But the liaison of Raphael with the formidable Julius produced a series of frescoes which rank as the most breathtaking creations of the High Renaissance. The decoration of the first room, the Stanza della Segnatura (the room where official documents were signed), occupied Raphael from the end of 1508 until 1511, and established his reputation as the foremost painter in Rome.

Around the time of its completion, Raphael entered into an arrangement with the Bolognese engraver Marcantonio Raimondi to make prints of some of his drawings which proved, usually, to consist of those he had made as preliminary studies for his works. Raphael realized that reproductive prints were a valuable means of popularizing his designs, as his best works – those in the Stanze – could only be seen by a handful of people within the Papal Court. The prints which Marcantonio made were very popular and contributed enormously to Raphael's growing reputation.

## WEALTH FROM THE WEALTHY

In 1511 Raphael carried out his first major project for Agostino Chigi, a wealthy Siennese banker, whose amorous adventures seem to have been matched only by Raphael's own. Chigi was a close friend and adviser to Julius II, and a man of great power who lived on a sumptuous scale. Between 1508 and 1511 he had a palatial villa built for himself by the architect Peruzzi, just outside the walls of Rome. Here he entertained in lavish style, astonishing his guests by throwing the silver plates into the nearby river at the end of every course. Unknown to them, nets had been

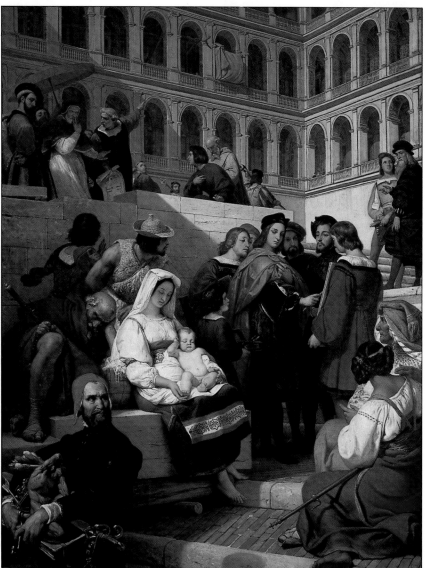

Horace Vernet/Raphael in the Vatican/Louvre, Paris

# La Fornarina

Raphael was famed for his amorous exploits, but little is known of the details – or whether they took place at all. Vasari, however, seemed in little doubt about Raphael's taste for romance. In his *Lives* he described Raphael's 'great fondness for women who he was always anxious to serve'. Accordingly, 'he was always indulging his sexual appetites; and in this matter his friends were probably more indulgent than they should have been'. Following Vasari's lead, various legends have sprung up around Raphael's love-life. *La Fornarina*, a voluptuous semi-nude portrait painted by Raphael in 1518, is reputedly his devoted mistress. On her arm she wears a band bearing the legend 'Raphael Urbinas'.

**La Fornarina**
*An X-ray examination has revealed that the background to this sensuous portrait (left) was originally an elaborate landscape, and the intimate tangle of myrtle, quince and laurel leaves Raphael painted in later may symbolize his deepening commitment to the woman. In Ingres' painting (right), it is the Fornarina who cradles the dying Raphael in her bosom.*

Raphael/La Fornarina/Palazzo Barberini, Rome

Ingres/Raphael and La Fornarina/Columbus Museum of Art, Ohio

countryman, Bramante, with responsibility for the fabric of St Peter's. He was also commissioned to begin a third apartment in the Vatican, the Stanza dell'Incendio – 'the room of fire' (p.99). At the same time, he was producing some of his most beautiful Madonnas, such as the *Madonna della Sedia* (p.82), and continued to be active as a portrait-painter. In July of that year, he wrote to his uncle Simone: 'I find my personal estate in Rome to be worth 3,000 gold ducats, with an income of 50 scudi a year, and as architect of St Peter's another 300 gold ducats, and on top of this I am paid for my work what I see fit to ask.'

## A PROPOSAL OF MARRIAGE

The same year, Raphael received a proposal of marriage. The influential Cardinal Bibbiena offered Raphael his niece Maria as a wife – a clear indication of Raphael's status and popularity at the Papal Court. Not wishing to offend Bibbiena, Raphael reluctantly agreed, but repeatedly delayed the wedding and Maria died before the marriage could be formalized. Renowned for his charming manner, Raphael is reputed to have had innumerable love-affairs, although his one lasting attachment seems to have been to a courtesan, the

Raphael/Triple Portrait with Leo X/Uffizi, Rome

**Pope Leo X**
*(left) Pope Leo X, like his predecessor Julius II, recognized Raphael's incomparable talent and not only ensured that he completed the painting of the Papal Apartments but engaged him on a host of other projects. This triple portrait of Leo X with two cardinals, including another member of the Medici family, Giulio, is one of Raphael's finest. Painted in 1518, it shows Raphael at the height of his powers, and the exquisite rendering of the cloths and the objects on the table drew from Vasari the comment: 'more lifelike than life itself'.*

legendary 'Fornarina'.

In 1515, Leo X appointed Raphael as Conservator of Roman Antiquities in the city. The Pope was anxious to preserve fragments of marble carrying classical inscriptions and instructed Raphael to ensure that none of these should be used in new building work. But Raphael took the task further, and embarked on a project to reconstruct the layout of Ancient Rome, as it had been in the Golden Age. It was a monumental task and together with his projects for the remodelling of St Peter's, diverted much of Raphael's attention from the business of painting. Nonetheless, he found time to design for Leo the cartoons for a set of 10 tapestries to adorn the lower walls of the Sistine Chapel (see p.83). These cartoons were sent to the workshop of Pieter Van Aelst in Brussels for weaving into tapestries.

Because of the growing demands on his time, Raphael began to make increasing use of assistants in his painting commissions. The decoration of the third Papal Apartment, the Stanza dell'Incendio, carried out between 1514 and 1517, was executed largely by Giulio Romano and Gianfrancesco Penni, after Raphael's designs. And his final project for Chigi, a series of frescoes for the vault of the second loggia in Chigi's villa, was carried out entirely by assistants, although the design was certainly Raphael's.

## THE ARTIST CRITICIZED

Raphael's rivals were quick to point out the inferior quality of the *Loggia of Cupid and Psyche*, as it was called. In January 1519, just after it had been completed, Leonardo Sellaio, a friend of Michelangelo's, wrote to the sculptor in Florence that the Loggia was 'shameful to a great artist, even worse than the last room in the Palace' (the Stanza dell'Incendio). Sellaio was hardly impartial, but even Vasari noted that the frescoes in the Loggia lacked Raphael's characteristic grace and sweetness, 'because he had them coloured by others, after his own designs'.

Nonetheless, when Raphael did turn his hand to painting, he proved triumphantly that his talent was still unsurpassed. In 1517 he was commissioned by Cardinal Giulio de' Medici to paint a panel of the *Transfiguration* (p.95), for his Cathedral Church at Narbonne, in France. The painting was barely finished when Raphael died, but when it was unveiled it was unanimously acclaimed, and confirmed Raphael's position as the supreme painter of his age.

It was to be his last major work, for in the spring of 1520, Raphael fell ill. Although Vasari claimed that his decline was brought on by an excessive bout of love-making, it seems more likely that he contracted a severe fever. He died on his birthday, 6 April, just 37 years of age. At his own request he was buried in the Pantheon, a classical building which he especially loved. In his honour, the *Transfiguration* was kept in Rome, in the church of San Pietro in Montorio.

Villa Farnesina, Rome

Scala

**Loggia of Cupid and Psyche**
(above) When Raphael agreed to paint this loggia in Agostini Chigi's villa in 1517, he was so much in demand that assistants actually executed the work.

**Raphael's burial place**
(below) Raphael so admired the Pantheon in Rome, the one great building to remain in use since Roman times, that he asked to be buried there.

T.E. Clark/Camerapix Hutchison Library

# A Courtly Art

**Raphael's harmonious compositions display a seemingly effortless skill and an apparently natural sense of ease and charm – qualities which reflect the elegant world of Castiglione's *Courtier.***

Today, Raphael is usually remembered as a painter of Madonnas. His enchanting variations on the theme of the Virgin and Child seem to us to sum up all that is best in Raphael's art. But the 16th-century view of Raphael was rather different. To the contemporary observer, the essence of Raphael's skill lay in his ability to depict every kind of figure, from the demure young mother to the frightened old man.

In his *Dialogue on Painting* published some 30 years after Raphael's death, the art critic Ludovico Dolce wrote: 'Michelangelo excells in one manner alone, that is in creating muscular nudes, skilfully foreshortened and in vigorous movement . . . But Raphael painted figures of every sort, some delicate, some fearsome and some vigorous'. Vasari expressed similar views, but added that Raphael realized that the good painter 'must be able to embellish his paintings with varied and unusual perspectives of buildings and landscapes, with lovely draperies . . . beautifully executed heads, and countless other things.'

In short, it was the range and variety of Raphael's work that was the secret of his genius. No-one doubted that Michelangelo was supreme in representing the heroic male nude. And in Leonardo's works, the discerning viewer could admire the intelligence and grandeur of his

Scala

Madonna della Sedia/Pitti, Florence

Réunion des Musées Nationaux

St Michael and the Dragon/Louvre, Paris

**Madonna of the Chair**
*(above) This, the most popular of Raphael's Madonnas, shows his mastery of the tondo, or circular form. The colours are an unusually vibrant mix of red, blue, orange and acid green.*

**St Michael and the Dragon (c.1505)**
*(left) This small canvas may have been painted for Guidobaldo, Duke of Urbino. Its 'courtly' theme – the triumph of virtue over evil – is complemented by the graceful figure style.*

underlying idea or *concetto*, even where the works were unfinished. But Raphael had mastered all aspects of painting, including a whole variety of figures which 'perfectly expressed the character of those they represented'.

It was partly this virtuosity which made Raphael the ideal 'courtly' artist. In his *Book of the Courtier*, Baldassare Castiglione had suggested that the courtier should be modestly accomplished in all pursuits and should not excel in one at the expense of the others. Raphael's art can be seen as the pictorial equivalent of this idea. His quiet mastery of every branch of painting, together with his courtly manner, ensured his popularity with the many cultivated men who were familiar with Castiglione's ideals.

Raphael developed his style by a painstaking process of observation and extraction, constantly studying the works of others and combining what he saw into his own distinctive style. Raphael was

Scala

never a mere imitator, and his drawings include few 'literal' copies of other artists' works. The motifs which inspired him were simply starting-points for his own ideas. By the time he came to draw them, they had already gone through various transformations, according to his particular needs.

In his early years, Raphael learnt much from Perugino, particularly in terms of composition. The carefully balanced groups of figures in his *Betrothal of the Virgin* (p.86), for example, clearly recall Perugino's famous *Donation of the Keys* (p.77). Raphael has also followed Perugino's technique of giving variety to his figures by contrasting the angles of their heads.

### LEONARDO'S INFLUENCE

Once in Florence, however, Raphael quickly left Perugino behind. Almost immediately, his works betray the influence of Leonardo, both in the softening of outlines and in the increased complexity of his compositions. His Madonnas of this period reflect his admiration for Leonardo's ability to combine the different movements of a small group of figures within a compact triangular shape. But the most important lesson that Raphael learnt from Leonardo was that the emotions must be expressed through the body as a whole.

The fruits of Raphael's Florentine years quickly became apparent in his paintings for the Stanza della Segnatura in the Vatican. Here, for the first time, Raphael displayed his ability to depict a

**'Auxiliary' cartoons**
*(below) In addition to full-scale cartoons, Raphael introduced the use of 'auxiliary' cartoons in his work. In these, the outline of the full-scale cartoon would be traced onto a fresh sheet of paper, and the heads or hands of the figures re-drawn in more detail. This study of two Apostles for the* Transfiguration *(p.95) shows the remarkable beauty of Raphael's drawing style.*

St Cecilia Altarpiece/Pinacoteca Nazionale, Bologna

**The St Cecilia Altarpiece (1513-14)**
*(above) Raphael painted several large altarpieces while he was in Rome, including this unconventional work dedicated to the patron saint of music.*

**The Miraculous Draught of Fishes**
*(below) This is one of ten coloured 'cartoons', or designs, that were sent to the weavers of Flanders to serve as models for the 'Raphael' tapestries.*

The Miraculous Draught of Fishes/Victoria and Albert Museum, London

Studies for the *Transfiguration*/Ashmolean Museum, Oxford

Study for *The Madonna of the Goldfinch*/Ashmolean Museum, Oxford

**Compositional study**
*(above) This vigorous pen and ink drawing for the*
Madonna of the Goldfinch *(p.88) shows Raphael's*
*admiration for Leonardo's pyramidal figure groupings.*

whole range of human types and emotions. In the
*School of Athens* and the *Disputà* (p.90 and p.98),
characters of every age, type and disposition move
and react with a seemingly infinite variety of
gestures, fused into two harmonious scenes.

Raphael achieved this balanced variety by a
process of painstaking preparation. The range of
Raphael's drawings is immense. For major
projects he made drawings for every stage of the
composition. These include rapid sketches of
heads and hands, detailed drapery studies and
numerous preliminary studies for groups of
figures, often drawn over and readjusted. Finally
there would be the full-scale cartoon which would
be pricked or traced through on to the surface to be
painted. In addition, Raphael sometimes used
secondary or 'auxiliary' cartoons, particularly for
the painting of heads and hands.

### 'NATURAL' GRACE

Despite Raphael's methodical approach, the
quality which impressed many of Raphael's
contemporaries was the apparent naturalness and
spontaneity of his works. The *School of Athens* and
the *Disputà* reveal nothing of the elaborate
preparation and planning which went into their
making. The visitor who walks into the 'Stanza'
seems to be confronted with a room full of
living beings, reading or conversing with
unselfconscious ease. This apparent artlessness or
'facility' was considered to be a supreme hallmark
of Raphael's art. And it was this quality, together

The Madonna of the Granduca/Pitti, Florence

## TRADEMARKS
# Lowered Eye-lids

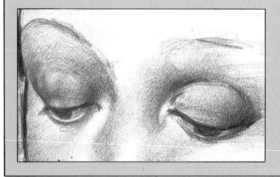

Raphael's Madonnas
are characterized by
their grace, sweetness
and modesty, qualities
which are emphasized
by their softened
features and gently
lowered eye-lids. Lost
in reverie, they gaze
quietly and tenderly
downwards.

**Madonna del Granduca (c.1506)**
*(left and detail above) By placing the Madonna and Child against a striking dark background, Raphael has created one of his simplest and most memorable images.*

with his virtuosity, which gave Raphael such a close affinity with the world of Castiglione's *Courtier*. For Castiglione, the courtier should do everything with an apparent naturalness and ease, a 'grace' which made everything seem effortless.

It was not simply the figures that onlookers admired in Raphael's 'Stanze'. Equal praise was reserved for his architectural backgrounds, and the variety of his 'special effects'. In describing the *Liberation of Saint Peter* (p.92) for example, Vasari wrote that Raphael 'depicted so skilfully the play of shadows, the flickering reflection of the lights and the vaporous glare of the torches within the surrounding gloom, that he can truly be said to be the master of every other painter.'

In his later works, Raphael's figures show a much greater robustness and solidity, probably reflecting the impact of Michelangelo's figures in the Sistine Chapel. As with all Raphael's work, however, this influence was absorbed gradually, and never took the form of direct copying. This process of assimilation is best illustrated by the *Transfiguration* (p.95). Here we find echoes of Leonardo's animated gestures and faces, Michelangelo's majestic figures, and the noble forms of classical sculpture. But the combination of all these elements is Raphael's own, and displays his unique narrative power. Each figure is a distinct individual, characterized by every detail of dress, feature and expression. Each one reacts in a totally different way, perfectly in keeping with his character. It is this variety, so vividly portrayed, that typifies the genius of Raphael.

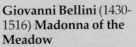

## COMPARISONS
# The Virgin and Child

Raphael's Madonnas are among the most appealing works of the Renaissance. Their peculiar sweetness and charm derive from a 15th-century Florentine tradition which replaced the stiff, hieratic images of Byzantine art with a much more endearing representation of the relationship between mother and child. In Renaissance Venice, however, the images have a greater solemnity, retaining the dignity of their Byzantine prototypes. Giovanni Bellini's Madonnas are especially moving interpretations of an extremely popular theme.

**Antonio Rossellino (1427-1479) Laughing Madonna and Child**
*(right) This delightful Florentine terracotta emphasizes the maternal aspect of the Virgin and Child theme. The little Christ Child is shown fully-clothed with his hand raised in blessing.*

**Giovanni Bellini (1430-1516) Madonna of the Meadow**
*(below) Bellini's serene vision shows the Madonna of Humility, seated on the ground. The naked Jesus lies sleeping across her lap, just as he will later lie across her knees in death.*

Victoria and Albert Museum, London

National Gallery, London

# Gallery

Raphael's early work was strongly influenced by his master Perugino: The Betrothal of the Virgin has all Perugino's serenity and grace, but also a new strength and dignity. But, in his Florentine period, it was Leonardo's work that affected him most deeply, both in the composition of his Madonna and Child paintings such as The

**The Betrothal of the Virgin** 1504
67" × 46" Brera, Milan

*This is the masterpiece of Raphael's early period, in which he showed that he had absorbed everything his master Perugino could teach him and then surpassed him in lucidity of composition and delicacy of touch. Joseph's staff has flowered, showing that he is favoured by God to be Mary's husband. On the right, one of Mary's rejected suitors breaks his staff over his knee.*

Madonna of the Goldfinch and in the ease and subtlety of his portraits, for example that of Agnolo Doni.

With his move to Rome, Raphael turned with astonishing assurance from small-scale works such as these to decorative painting in the most heroic manner. The School of Athens and the Liberation of Saint Peter are two of the most sublime frescoes he painted in the Vatican.

In his later career, Raphael was so overworked that he relied heavily on assistants. But in paintings from his own hand, such as the Sistine Madonna or the Transfiguration, his work continued to evolve in subtlety of expression.

Scala

**Portrait of Agnolo Doni** *c.1506*
23¾″ × 17¾″ Pitti Palace, Florence

*The portrait of Agnolo Doni and a companion picture of his wife are the outstanding portraits Raphael produced before his move to Rome in 1508. Vasari records that Doni 'although tight in other matters, spent willingly, although saving what he could, on pictures and statues, with which things he was much delighted'. Raphael has admirably caught this shrewdness.*

**The Madonna of the Goldfinch** *1507*
42¼″ × 30¼″ Uffizi, Florence

*During the period when he was based in Florence (1504-8), Raphael painted several lovely pictures of the Virgin and Child that show the influence of Leonardo in their pyramidical compositions. The goldfinch is a symbol of Christ's Passion: according to legend it acquired its distinctive red spot when it pulled a thorn from His head and was splashed with His blood.*

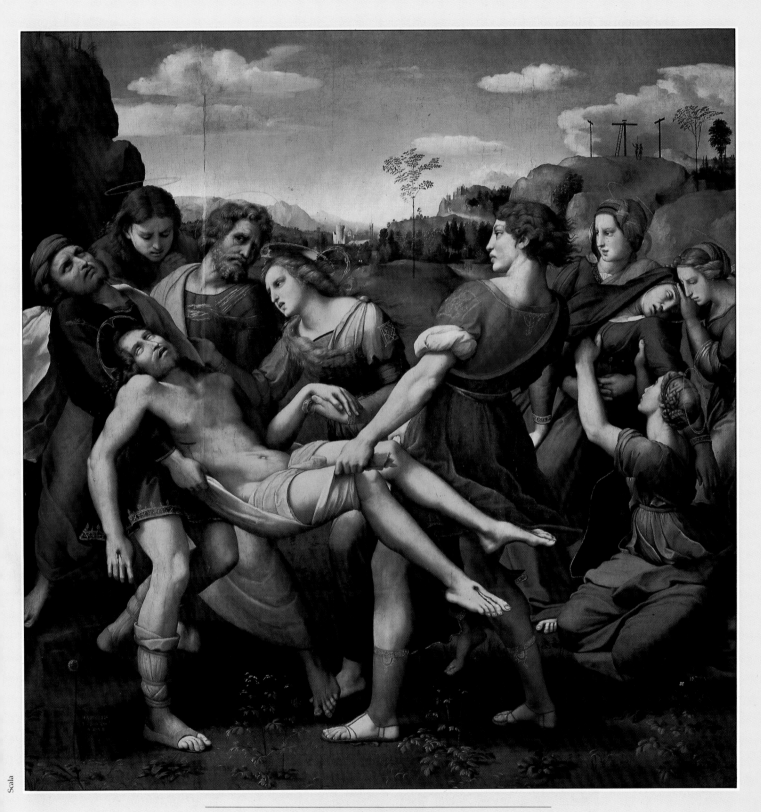

Scala

**The Entombment** *1507*
72½″ × 69¼″ Borghese Gallery, Rome

*A prestigious private commission for a church in Perugia, this was
Raphael's first attempt at a dramatic multi-figure composition, and as
the numerous surviving preparatory drawings show, he took immense
pains over its planning. Many critics consider that his inexperience
shows in a lack of unity, but there is no denying the beauty of the
individual figures and the landscape background.*

**The School of Athens** *1509-11*
base 303" Stanza della Segnatura, Vatican

*By common consent, this majestic fresco, in which heroic figures move serenely in an architectural setting of the utmost grandeur, is one of the supreme works of the Renaissance. The painting's familiar title dates only from the 17th century: the scene shows an imaginary assembly of the greatest ancient philosophers (Aristotle and Plato are in the centre) and symbolizes the rational pursuit of truth.*

Scala

**The Liberation of Saint Peter** *1513-4*
base 260″ Stanza d' Eliodoro, Vatican

*This is one of the most imaginative night scenes in the history of art, the different light sources – the torch, the moonlit sky and the angel's supernatural aura – being beautifully observed and differentiated. Raphael has used the pictorial convention known as continuous representation to show two events from the same narrative in one painting: in the centre the angel rouses the sleeping St Peter and on the right leads him out of prison. The painting has been interpreted as an allegory of the deliverance of Italy from French invaders, who were expelled in 1512. It has always been regarded as one of Raphael's greatest works, and in an 18th-century English guide book to Italy was referred to as 'incontestably the finest Night-Piece in the world'.*

**The Sistine Madonna** *c.1513*
104¼″ × 77¼″ Gemäldegalerie, Dresden

*Raphael's most original painting of the Virgin and Child, this
celebrated altarpiece has for centuries been endlessly copied and
reproduced. It was painted for the church of St Sixtus in Piacenza; St
Sixtus is on the left (represented with the features of Julius II) and on
the right is St Barbara. Between them float the Virgin and Child – a
celestial vision of surpassing loveliness.*

Scala

**The Transfiguration** *1517-20*
159½″ × 109½″ Vatican Picture Gallery

*Raphael's last great work, this painting was unfinished at his death and
was completed by his studio. It was an important commission for
Narbonne Cathedral and Raphael spared no effort to achieve what
Vasari called 'the ultimate perfection'. Two related biblical episodes are
shown: above, Christ rises between Moses and Elijah; below, a boy
possessed by evil spirits is taken to the disciples to be cured.*

THE MAKING OF A MASTERPIECE

# The School of Athens
## (Stanza della Segnatura)

The 'School of Athens' is the most famous fresco in the Stanza della Segnatura (p.98) – the papal apartment decorated by Raphael. Its title was coined by a French 17th-century travel guide, in a somewhat misleading attempt to identify the subject-matter. The key to the true meaning of the fresco is provided by the ceiling decoration and, in particular, by the lovely allegorical figure situated directly above. She is accompanied by the inscription *'Causarum Cognitio'* – the definition of Philosophy, being 'the knowledge of things through their highest causes'. She holds two volumes, inscribed *'Moralis'* and *'Naturalis'* – the main branches of philosophy, which are represented by Aristotle and Plato below. The other three frescoes in the rooms, representing Poetry, Law and Theology, are intimately linked with the concept of Philosophy in Renaissance thought. Each of these disciplines leads to a revelation of 'higher' truths and ultimately to a knowledge of the Divine.

'Philosophy is the greatest of the gifts which the immortal Gods bestowed on mortal man.'
Toscanella

**The Stanza della Segnatura**
*(above) Raphael decorated the walls and ceiling of this modest room in the Vatican between 1508 and 1511. The 'School of Athens' was probably the third fresco to be completed.*

**'Philosophy'**
*(right) The robe of the allegorical figure above the fresco is decorated with flowers on the hem, fish on the skirt and flowers on the bodice, symbolizing the branches of moral, natural and contemplative philosophy.*

### 'Geometry'
(left) The various groups of figures in the composition may illustrate the seven Liberal Arts – Geometry and Astronomy are clearly represented. Here, admiring pupils watch a demonstration by Euclid.

### Plato and Aristotle
(below) These two ancient philosophers represent natural and moral philosophy. Plato, holding his book the Timaeus, points upwards, while Aristotle, holding the Ethics, gestures before him.

Albertina, Vienna

### Preliminary study
(left) This delicate silverpoint drawing represents one of the many stages in the evolution of the fresco. The poses and varied attitudes of the figures have already been established and Raphael has moved on to a study of the pattern and fall of the draperies.

### Full-scale cartoon
(left) An enormous cartoon, some 9' by 26', survives for the 'School of Athens'. It shows that the brooding figure in the foreground was an after-thought: Raphael may have added him after seeing Michelangelo's monumental figure-style on the Sistine Ceiling – only a few rooms away.

### Architectural eloquence
(right) Raphael's philosophers move freely in a mathematically constructed interior, organized around a central vanishing point.

Ambrosiana, Milan

Berry/Fallon Design

# Stanza della Segnatura

In 1508, Pope Julius II gave Raphael his first major commission – to decorate the ceiling and walls of the Stanza della Segnatura, one of the papal apartments in the Vatican. This room was designed as the Pope's library and was also where he signed the decrees of the ecclesiastical court – hence its name. The scheme of the decoration starts on the ceiling, with the personification, in the form of four beautiful women, of Theology, Philosophy, Poetry and the Science of Law. The theme is then expanded and amplified on each of the four walls: the *School of Athens*, Raphael's masterpiece, illustrates Philosophy; the *Disputà*, Theology; the *Parnassus*, Poetry; the *Wall of Justice*, Law. Raphael completed the room within three years, and the reaction to his work established him as one of the greatest artists of the Renaissance.

**The Parnassus**
(*top and detail above*) *A master of figural arrangement, Raphael designed this glorification of ancient and contemporary poets and writers to fit naturally around a large window. The detail shows Apollo's beautiful Muses.*

**The Disputà (Disputation on the Sacrament)**
(*above left and left*) *In this fresco, which faces the* School of Athens, *theologians contemplate the mystery of the Eucharist. Many preparatory drawings have survived, which enable us to see how Raphael worked.*

# Stanza d' Eliodoro

Following the great success of the Stanza della Segnatura, Raphael was commissioned to fresco another room, the Stanza d'Eliodoro – so called because of its main fresco the *Expulsion of Heliodorus from the Temple* (below). In contrast to the conceptual nature of the Segnatura frescoes, the feeling of this room is one of history and drama. The other frescoes are the *Mass of Bolsena*, the *Liberation of Saint Peter* and the *Meeting of Attila with St Leo the Great*.

**Mass of Bolsena**
*(detail right) This right-hand section of the fresco shows Julius II's papal guard of Swiss soldiers. They were officially termed protectors of the church in 1512 and awarded with their characteristic sword and beret.*

# Stanza dell' Incendio

Raphael started work in 1514 on a third room – the Stanza dell' Incendio – this time for Pope Leo X. This was a busy time for Raphael, however, and he could not give his full attention to all the frescoes in the room. The only one which is entirely his design, although not wholly executed by him, is the *Fire in the Borgo*. The others, the *Battle of Ostia*, the *Coronation of Charlemagne* and the *Oath of Leo III* are the work of Raphael's assistants and are markedly inferior in style.

**The Fire in the Borgo**
*(left and detail above) This fresco depicts an incident in the life of Pope Leo IV when, with a blessing from St Peter, he miraculously conquered a raging fire.*

# The Ruins of Ancient Rome

**After the fall of the Roman Empire, the glories of the capital suffered
a thousand years of neglect until Renaissance popes and patrons
discovered their ancient heritage.**

The Rome that Raphael knew bore little resemblance to the bustling capital of today. Nor was it in any sense the grand city of ancient Rome. That lay smashed, decayed and largely buried under the rubble of more than a thousand years of continuous inhabitation since the Empire's fall.

16th-century Rome was very much a medieval town, surrounded by walls and consisting largely of a jumble of unplanned and poorly built houses, with a scattering of palaces and churches. In some areas it was overcrowded and unhealthy, with narrow, refuse-strewn streets. Yet in others, it was empty and overgrown, like the derelict land found in modern cities around redundant docks or factories. The city walls followed the perimeter laid down by the Romans, and the area enclosed was far larger than the city now required.

**Monuments to the past**
*(above) Dwarfing present-day visitors, these partly reconstructed ruins of the forum area were used for grazing cattle by the Renaissance Romans.*

**Papal influence**
*(left) Pope Nicholas V brought Florentine artists and architects to Rome to decorate the Vatican, where they stimulated new interest in classical art.*

Scala

State Archives, Siena

But the ancient capital had not just been larger. It had also been immensely rich, and full of huge and magnificent buildings. All over the city there were signs of this past splendour. From the wasteland protruded battered walls of brick and cement, weathered lumps of concrete, overgrown and cracked columns, and shattered fragments of inscribed marble.

The walls of the city included whole sections of Roman masonry, and scattered among the chaotic medieval buildings were surviving monuments, still splendid enough to dominate their surroundings. The Colosseum, for example, was still one of the largest structures in Europe, although a complete ruin. The Pantheon, a magnificent circular temple, was still in use as a church. Its vast dome had been built using a sophisticated construction method beyond the understanding of Renaissance architects.

In unassuming areas of the city stood structures such as the Quirinal monument, a dilapidated obelisk flanked by equestrian statues. A few hundred yards away was Trajan's Column, its lower part still underground but most of its processional spiral of sculpture visible.

Beyond this lay the Arch of Constantine, emerging from the soil of the Forum, with the Palatine Hill studded with giant brick structures behind. For generations, Rome's inhabitants had seen such ruins as little more than a useful source of building material, to be pillaged at will.

During the Middle Ages, Rome slowly began to

*Image Bank/Obremski*

*Spectrum Colour Library*

**Arch of Constantine**
*(above) The magnificent reliefs on this arch were familiar to the artists and sculptors of the Renaissance. The arch itself was constructed early in the fourth century.*

inspired them. Rich Florentine collectors, such as the Medici, snapped up any ancient sculpture that happened to come to the surface.

The real change came with Alexander VI, the Borgia prince who was Pope from 1492 to 1503. In carrying out a considerable programme of restoration of the buildings under his control, he insisted that anything excavated that was of interest became his personal property. From the Castel Sant'Angelo, for example, he acquired a colossal bust of the Emperor Hadrian.

## ROME RESTORED

In his successor, Julius II, Rome found a ruler of greatness to match its glorious past. Employing artists and architects of the calibre of Michelangelo, Raphael and Bramante, he proceeded to turn the decayed city into a glorious wonder; it was to express in stone and in paint the majesty of papal power and authority.

The classical style of ancient art was ideally suited to this aim, especially as it expressed continuity with the church founded in Rome by St Peter. Julius decided this was the style in which his

*Image Bank/Larry Dale Gordon*

grow as the new centre of Christian Europe. But for much of the time the popes, although nominally Bishops of Rome, lived elsewhere – even, for a considerable time, at Avignon in southern France. And it was not until the 15th century that signs of renewal were seen: in 1420, the popes returned for good, and began the painful process of restoring the city.

Nicholas V, Pope from 1447 to 1455, brought artists and architects from Florence – a richer and more advanced centre – to beautify his Vatican palace. They were glad to come. Rome held great fascination for the Florentines. Even in earlier years they had been coming to investigate the surviving Roman art with its classical style that so

**An emperor's bust**
*This huge head of Constantine was discovered between 1484 and 1492.*

**Rome mapped**
*Fulvio, basing his research on work begun by Raphael, published this map – one of the most scholarly attempts at a topographical study of Ancient Rome – in his Antiquitates Urbi (1527).*

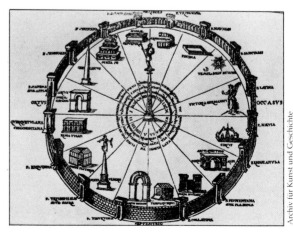

*Archiv für Kunst und Geschichte*

M. Pucciarelli

make room for the new. Even St Peter's basilica, the holiest shrine in the west, was virtually razed to the ground.

Julius's successor after 1513, Leo X, continued the massive building programmes but tempered them with greater concern for the remains. In 1515 he asked Raphael to carry out a complete survey of the ancient city and its monuments.

There were precedents for this. For example, the Florentine architect Brunelleschi had wanted to measure the Roman ruins in the 1430s; in 1446, Flavio Biondo had published *Roma Instaurata* which was an attempt to reconstruct the appearance of the city from surviving ancient texts.

But Raphael's task went much further, and to it he brought an extraordinarily modern approach. First he buried himself in the ancient literature, and then he went out and systematically measured and drew the remains. He conceived the project on a vast scale, but only completed his work for one of the 14 regions of the city by the time of his death.

In a celebrated letter to Pope Leo, Raphael

painters, sculptors and architects should work.

On becoming Pope, he already had a fine collection of ancient sculpture. At its centre was the priceless statue of Apollo, and in 1506 he added to this the fabulous Laocoon group which he bought for a huge price from a Roman citizen who found it buried in his vineyard.

## A SHRINE OF SCULPTURE

These and other ancient statues were grouped in a special garden court designed by Bramante, with orange trees and streams, and built for Julius in the Belvedere – a summer residence on the edge of the Vatican. Bramante also built a long, three-tiered gallery to connect the Belvedere to the Vatican, the start of a huge project which was never completed. The Pope's sculpture court became a major inspiration to artists. For hundreds of years it was almost a place of pilgrimage.

In 1506, Julius began work on St Peter's, then in a perilously ruinous condition. But although this and his other major projects did much to stimulate interest in ancient art, paradoxically they also did much to destroy what remained of it. The ancient monuments were increasingly plundered for their stone and were, quite simply, cleared away to

**The Golden House**
*(above) This section of Nero's fabled Golden House – his sumptuous palace – with its witty trompe-l'oeil and delicately executed wall paintings was one of the wonders that Raphael was familiar with. He was greatly influenced by the murals and he used several of their decorative motifs.*

**A divine statue**
*This handsome marble of the Roman god Apollo was one of the treasures of Raphael's patron, Pope Julius II. Discovered between 1490 and 1500, Julius eventually moved it to a specially designed garden in the Belvedere, the Bishop of Rome's summer residence.*

**A triumph of architecture**
*(right) The Pantheon was the most famous standing building surviving from the ancient days of Rome. The secrets of its construction defied the Renaissance builders and the beauties of its interior were legendary.*

M. Pucciarelli

Scala

outlined his method and his broad findings. He and his assistants also produced detailed drawings of several monuments such as Trajan's Column (below). A drawing by Raphael's own hand of a horse of the Quirinal monument (right) shows an almost archaeological precision in delineating the measurements and the joints in the stone.

But Raphael could not stem the tide of destruction caused by the demand for building stone, and in the first paragraphs of his letter to Leo he pleaded in vain: 'The very persons who should have been the special champions of the desolate remains of ancient Rome have shown themselves the most forward in robbing and injuring her'.

Fortunately, his work was continued after his death – although with much less precision – by Andrea Fulvio who had accompanied him on some of his visits to the ancient sites. In 1527, seven years after Raphael's death, Fulvio published his *Antiquitates Urbi*, a full topographical study of the Eternal City.

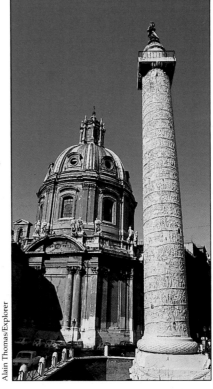

**Raphael, archaeologist**
(above) In 1515, Pope Leo X asked Raphael to make a survey of Ancient Rome. Raphael's meticulous approach to the study of ancient Rome and its work of art anticipated the techniques of modern archaeology. Not only does this drawing of one of the Horses of Monte Cavallo show the great pains he went to in the accurate measurement of the dimensions of the sculpture, but it also shows his artistic mastery. Sadly, Raphael died shortly after starting his archaeological study of the Ancient capital.

**Trajan's column**
(above and detail left) The warlike Trajan was the last emperor to make dramatic enlargements to the boundaries of Rome's domain by conquest. In his reign, which ended in 117 AD, he fought on many of the fronts of the by now mighty Empire. His military prowess was celebrated by this famous column. Its sculpture (left) was familiar to the Renaissance artists in Rome; the column was then half buried and the reliefs accessible at eye level.

# A Year in the Life 1509

**While Raphael worked in the Vatican, his patron – the warrior-pope Julius II – was embroiled in war again. And as the Pope manipulated an unholy alliance with Spain and France, England's new king, Henry VIII, established a more intimate partnership with the King of Spain's daughter. But neither alliance lasted.**

In 1509, Raphael, was at work on his great frescoes, the *Disputà* and *The School of Athens*, which proclaim the truths made manifest by revelation and reason. Julius II is shown in the *Disputà* in the guise of an earlier pontiff, Pope Gregory the Great, and as such he is seated close to the altar beneath the enthroned Christ.

But that year Julius's preoccupations were of a less spiritual nature as he had become part of a predatory military alliance directed against Venice. This was not out of character: although the Vicar of Christ – and an old man – Julius was always ready to buckle on armour and lead troops to war.

Since he had assumed the papal tiara in 1503, Julius had devoted himself to recovering and extending papal territories. He successfully drove Cesare Borgia from Italy, conquered

**A founding father**
*(above) Louis XII of France (1462-1515) was known as the Father of the People by the citizens of Tours. He is said to have founded the city of Le Havre in 1509 between military expeditions to Italy. The illustration shows him leaving Alexandria to chastise Genoa.*

**A busy year for Erasmus**
*(right) In 1509, Desiderius Erasmus (c.1466-1536) the humanist and scholar, divided his time between lecturing on Greek in Cambridge, and completing his book* Praise of Folly. *This satire drew on classical and medieval sources, and had lasting success.*

**Gift to learning**
*(left) Brasenose College, Oxford, was founded in 1509 thanks to the generosity of William Smyth, Bishop of Lincoln.*

**Coronation and marriage**
*(right) 1509 was a momentous year for Henry Tudor (1491-1547). He acceded to the throne on the death of his father, and he forged an alliance with Spain by marrying his brother Arthur's widow, Catharine of Aragon, to whom he had been betrothed for six years.*

Perugia and Bologna and then determined to force the Venetian Republic to relinquish control of its subject-town in the northern Italian region of Romagna.

Since Julius was not strong enough to challenge Venice on his own, he persuaded the major European powers to aid his conquest. In 1508, the Holy Roman Emperor Maximilian, Louis XII of France and King Ferdinand of Spain all joined the Pope in the League of Cambrai. The coalition aimed to despoil Venice of all her mainland territories, and share them out between them.

It was a bad year for the Venetians. On 14 March, even before war broke out, a spark ignited the magazine of the famous Arsenal, causing a tremendous explosion and a terrible fire. 'I saw many corpses drawn from the ruins', wrote an eye-witness, 'some without heads and some in pieces'. The disaster

weakened Venetian morale as well as depleting her stock of war materials. Still, when Pope Julius excommunicated Venice as a rebel against the Holy Church, and a friend to the infidel Turk, the Venetians were not worried: they simply declined to publish the papal bull. Such politically motivated excommunications were commonplace, and normally ignored unless backed by force.

## VENETIAN DEFEAT

But on this occasion the French supplied the force. In May, they fought the Venetians at the village of Agnadello while pouring rain turned the battlefield into a quagmire. Half the Venetian army took part and found itself surrounded and cut to

Lambert Barnard/Bishop Sherburne and Henry VIII

**The destruction of a historic city**
*(above) In 1509 the ancient city of Byzantium – then known as Constantinople – was hit by an earthquake, which devastated countless works of art. Now Istanbul occupies the site.*

**Wise foolishness**
*Sebastian Brant's verse satire* The Ship of Fools *was translated from German into English in 1509, and influenced Erasmus among many others. Dürer was possibly the illustrator.*

pieces; the other half – mercenaries who were reliable as long as the pay was good and things were going well – quietly melted away. With French and Imperial troops advancing, the Spaniards taking over the Venetian cities of southern Italy, and the Pope making good his claims to the Romagna, the Venetian state was on the point of collapse.

## TURNCOAT PONTIFF

However, once Julius II had got what he wanted – the control of the cities in the Romagna – he had second thoughts about his overmighty allies. They had played their part, but he had no intention that all of northern Italy should fall into the hands of foreigners. And soon he left the alliance, and decided

to forgive Venice. Within a few months Julius, now allied to Venice, was in arms again and working towards a new 'Holy League' that would drive out the impious French invaders.

While the Pope had been manipulating his political allegiances to consolidate his power, in 1509 England's new King – Henry VIII – began his reign with a similarly motivated alliance. Julius had joined with King Ferdinand in the League of Cambrai; Henry made a more long-lasting partnership with his brother's widow, and Ferdinand's youngest daughter, Catherine of Aragon. But though the Pope could pull out of the League once it had served his purpose, Henry had more difficulty extricating himself from his marriage. Some 20 years later it led to England's dramatic break with the Church of Rome, and the birth of the Church of England.

**The passing of Freedom**
*(below) This miniature shows the herbs and unleavened bread associated with the Jewish Passover, the Festival of Freedom. But in 1509, Maximilian I endorsed the persecution of Jews in Germany by suppressing their books.*

**Doctors of the short robe**
*(below right) In 1509 much minor surgery was performed by barbers, whose red and white pole symbolised blood and bandages. It was beneath university-trained surgeons, known as doctors of the long robe, to do such things as lance abcesses.*

**Scourge of Geneva**
*(right) John Calvin was born in this year in Picardy, and during his 55 years he had an enormous influence in Geneva, the centre of the Reformation. He rationalised Protestantism and subjected the citizens of Geneva to rigorous moral discipline.*

IOHANNES · CALVINVS ·
ANNO · ÆTATIS ·53·
·B·

School of Van Eyck/The Jewish Passover

Peter Newark's Historical Pictures

Mary Evans Picture Library

Archiv für Kunst und Geschichte

# TITIANVS . P.

## c.1485-1576

The greatest painter of the Venetian School, Titian dominated art in the city during its most glorious period. He trained in the studio of Giovanni Bellini, the leading painter of the previous generation, and when Bellini died in 1516, Titian was left without a serious rival in Venice – a position he maintained until his death 60 years later. Europe's royalty and aristocracy also eagerly sought his work.

Unlike many of the other giants of Renaissance art, who spread their talents widely, Titian was purely a painter. He left a huge body of work and excelled in virtually every subject – his masterpieces include erotic mythologies, profoundly moving religious works and some of the finest portraits ever painted. When he died, aged about 90, he was a rich man and the most famous artist in Europe.

# Venice's Supreme Painter

**Titian dominated Venetian art for 60 years. His superlative skill and ability to charm won him patronage and friendship from princes, a pope and the powerful Holy Roman Emperor, King Charles V.**

## Key Dates

**c.1485** born in Pieve di Cadore, Italy

**1508** collaborates with Giorgione on the Fondaco dei Tedeschi, Venice

**1516** becomes official painter to the Republic of Venice; begins painting *The Assumption of the Virgin;* visits court of Ferrara

**1529** first introduced to Charles V

**1533** appointed official painter to Charles V; granted rank of Count Palatine and Knight of the Golden Spur

**1545** visits Pope Paul III in Rome

**1548** spends nine months with the Imperial court at Augsburg; meets Philip II in Milan

**1554** begins series of 'poesie' for Philip II

**1576** dies in Venice

Tiziano Vecellio was born in Pieve di Cadore, a small town in the Italian Alps which had become part of the Republic of Venice in 1421. His father Gregorio di Conte Vecellio was a respected town official, whose wife Lucia bore him three more children, Francesco, Orsola and Caterina.

The date of Titian's birth has always been a matter of speculation. Towards the end of his career he himself tended to exaggerate his age to enlist the sympathy of his patrons – a letter to King Philip II of Spain implied that he had been born in 1476 or 1477. Yet some of his admirers and biographers, including Giorgio Vasari, the Florentine artist and critic, suggested a much later date of c.1490, probably in order to surround his early career with an aura of precocity. The truth is probably somewhere between these two extremes – a date around 1485 appears far more likely in the light of Titian's career.

### A VENETIAN APPRENTICESHIP

The young Titian and his brother Francesco were duly sent to Venice to stay with their uncle and to learn a trade. Here he studied with the mosaicist Sebastiano Zuccati, and then with the painter Gentile Bellini, but finding him too old-fashioned, Titian transferred to the workshop of Gentile's brother, Giovanni.

He could not have made a better choice. His new master was one of the outstanding painters of Italy. He had developed the recently imported

**Colourful Venice**
*(right) Titian first moved to Venice as a young boy, and remained based there for the rest of his long life. The city's waterways create an intensity of light and colour which is reflected in Titian's painting.*

Mirco Decet

**Titian's birthplace**
*(left) Titian was born in the small town of Pieve di Cadore in the Italian Alps, about 70 miles from Venice. His family home is now open to the public.*

## An early work

*(right)* The Jealous Husband *(1511) was one of three frescoes on the theme of the miracles of St Anthony which Titian painted for the Scuola di Sant'Antonio in Padua. These are the artist's only surviving frescoes.*

Scuola di Sant'Antonio, Padua

After Titian/Metropolitan Museum of Art, New York

foreign traders was that of the Germans. Their huge warehouse, the Fondaco dei Tedeschi, stood on the Grand Canal next to the old bridge of the Rialto. Here the young Titian, an independent master in 1508, joined with the Venetian painter Giorgione to decorate the facades with allegorical frescoes. According to Vasari, many people mistook Titian's work for Giorgione's and complimented Giorgione on his improved style. Giorgione was so upset that 'until Titian had completely finished and his share in the work had become general knowledge, he would hardly show himself out of doors.'

These frescoes have since crumbled in the damp climate of the lagoon, but the co-operation between the two painters extended far beyond this one commission. With the older Giorgione taking the leading role, the two artists explored new techniques of oil painting, applying the heavy, undiluted medium directly to a coarse canvas.

In 1513 Titian received an invitation from Pope Leo X to visit Rome. This was a unique chance to work alongside Raphael and Michelangelo, yet Titian – who was deeply attached to his Venetian roots and who remained, throughout his life, highly reluctant to travel – turned it down. He continued to work for his local patrons – religious institutions and members of the patrician class

technique of oil painting to supreme perfection, and by the time Titian joined him, Giovanni Bellini was famous for his colouring and for the glowing effects of light and atmosphere in his altarpieces and smaller devotional images.

Venice around 1500 was at the height of its power, one of the richest and biggest cities in Europe. It dominated a vast empire from Cyprus in the eastern Mediterranean to the Italian mainland. An independent republic with an unequalled history of internal peace, justice and freedom, it was the envy of the rest of Italy.

The city attracted merchants from all over the world, and perhaps the largest group among these

## Original setting

*(above) Titian's huge altarpiece, the* Assumption of the Virgin *(1516) is still in its original setting in the church of Santa Maria dei Frari, Venice.*

## First princely patron

*(left) In 1517 Duke Alfonso d'Este commissioned Titian to contribute to a series of mythological paintings for the lavish study which adjoined his castle in Ferrara.*

# The Legend of Giorgione

In 1508 Titian worked alongside Giorgione on murals for the Fondaco dei Tedeschi, a warehouse on Venice's Grand Canal. At this point their painting styles were so close that their works have often been confused. Attributions are particularly difficult, since the life of Giorgione is shrouded in mystery: only a handful of works are accepted as his.

Vasari described Giorgione as a romantic and musical young man, and considered him to be one of the founders of 'modern' painting. He mainly produced small oil paintings for private collectors, noted for their obscure subject matter and poetic mood.

John Sims

Scala

**Giorgione (c.1478-1510)**
(left) Giorgione was born in Castelfranco in the Veneto, where this statue stands.

**The Tempest**
(right) This is one of Giorgione's few surviving documented works. His use of landscape and mood as the main 'subject' was revolutionary, and had a profound influence on Titian's art.

Accademia, Venice

such as Niccolò Aurelio, the Great Chancellor of the Republic, a humanist and collector, who commissioned *Sacred and Profane Love* (p.122).

The call to Rome, however, clearly enhanced Titian's reputation, and after Giovanni Bellini's death in 1516 he succeeded his old master as official painter to the Republic. His first major public commission was the altarpiece of the *Assumption of the Virgin* (p.124), painted for the high altar of Sta Maria dei Frari, one of the major churches in Venice.

In the same year he received an invitation from Alfonso d'Este, Duke of Ferrara, who was to become one of Titian's most important patrons. Through Alfonso, Titian also came into contact with the princely rulers of Mantua and Urbino, whose courts prided themselves on their sophisticated culture and humanist learning.

Over the next two decades, Titian established relationships of friendship and mutual respect with this new group of patrons. Although he continued to work for the Venetian churches, he was much more interested in princely patronage. Quite apart from the status this brought him, he could command far higher fees.

After Titian's first visit to Ferrara, the artist began a series of mythological paintings for the Duke's new study, the Camerino d'Alabastro.

**An elegant patron**
(right) This striking portrait of Federico Gonzaga, Duke of Mantua was probably painted in 1529. An elegant and highly cultivated man, Federico was both Titian's friend and patron, and was responsible for introducing the artist to the Emperor Charles V.

Giraudon

Prado, Madrid

These included *Bacchus and Ariadne* (p.125) and *The Andrians* (p.114). Titian's notoriously slow progress and his dismissive and casual responses to the threats and commands issued via the Duke's agent in Venice, provoked the prince to outbursts of fury. Yet after the death of Leonardo in 1519 and that of Raphael in 1520, and with Michelangelo devoting his time almost exclusively to sculpture and architecture, there was no one to challenge Titian's role as the leading painter in Italy. If the Duke wanted to keep the painter's services, he had to be as patient as any other patron.

## FRIEND OF PRINCES

It was not just his professional success which helped Titian to bridge the social gap which existed between painter and prince. He was by all accounts a man of grace and charm, attractive and interesting in conversation. In 1532, Alfonso's nephew, Duke Federico II Gonzaga wrote to his friend Titian begging him to come and stay with him in Mantua, and when the master finally undertook the journey to Rome in 1545, he stopped briefly in Pesaro where he was received by Duke Guidobaldo della Rovere of Urbino with royal honours, and provided with an escort for the rest of his journey.

By that time the princes were flattered to be associated with the great master. Not only was he on his way to Rome as the guest of Pope Paul III Farnese, he was also court painter to Charles V, Emperor of the Holy Roman Empire and King of Spain, the most powerful man of the century. It was no secret that Titian was on friendly, even intimate terms with Charles.

Capodimonte, Naples

**Pope Paul III**
*(above) Titian travelled to Rome in 1545 at the invitation of Pope Paul, and in the expectation of obtaining a church income for his son Pomponio. There he painted this (unfinished) portrait of the frail, ageing Pope flanked by his grandsons Cardinal Alessandro and Ottavio Farnese.*

**A lost masterpiece**
*(left) This engraving is a copy of Titian's* Death of St Peter Martyr *(1530) which was destroyed by fire in 1867. Vasari described the original altarpiece as the 'most celebrated, the greatest work . . . that Titian in all his life had ever done'.*

Their first meeting, arranged by Federico Gonzaga after Charles' coronation in Bologna in 1529, had been less than successful. The Emperor was rumoured to have paid Titian only one ducat for his portrait, and Gonzaga had to contribute the remaining 149 ducats of the agreed price.

Yet, after another meeting in Bologna three years later, when Titian painted further portraits of the Emperor, Charles' attitude to him changed dramatically. He issued a patent appointing Titian as his exclusive portrait-painter, praising his exquisite talents, likening him to Apelles who had painted Alexander the Great, and elevating him – in an unprecedented fashion for a painter – to the rank of Count Palatine and Knight of the Golden Spur, with all the privileges of knighthood and nobility, including the right of entrance to Court.

To serve the Emperor, Titian had to overcome his aversion to travelling. In 1548 he even had to cross the Alps in mid winter to spend the busiest nine months of his life in Germany, hectically painting portraits of Charles, his family, the princes of Germany and the members of the Imperial Court, all of whom had gathered for a session of the *Reichstag* in Augsburg.

When Charles abdicated and withdrew to a monastery, he took with him a number of paintings by Titian. His son and successor on the

Titian/Lavinia with a Tray of Fruit/Staatliche Gemäldegalerie, Berlin

**Titian's model daughter**
*(left) Titian often used his daughter Lavinia as a model.
In a variant of this work, she appears in the same pose,
but as Salome – carrying the Baptist's head on a platter.*

urgent need to provide for the future of his
children. His wife Cornelia had died in 1530,
leaving him with two sons and one daughter
(another daughter having died in infancy). The
children were brought up by his sister Orsola who
looked after his household until her death in 1550.
The eldest son, Pomponio, was to become a
clergyman, but as he led the careless and
dissipated life of a well-to-do young gentleman, he
more than once incurred his father's displeasure.
Orazio, on the other hand, followed his father's
footsteps and joined his workshop.

From 1531, Titian lived and worked in a large
house in Biri Grande, on the eastern edge of
Venice, opposite the islands of San Michele and
Murano. This was then an almost rural part of
Venice, with gardens overlooking the lagoon. In
his house and garden Titian entertained his friends
and visitors with a lavish hospitality which was
quite at odds with his notorious greed and his self-
proclaimed poverty.

## SCHOLARLY FRIENDS

Titian's own education as a young boy cannot have
been very substantial. Yet throughout his life he
attracted the friendship and admiration of some of
the most learned men of his time. His first
invitation to Rome in 1513 was instigated by the
eminent humanist Cardinal Pietro Bembo, and it
was said that the great poet Andrea Navagero
persuaded him to turn it down.

When in 1527 Spanish and German troops
sacked Rome, many artists, poets and humanists
fled to Venice, which was famous for its republican

Spanish throne, Philip II, also succeeded his father
as Titian's loyal patron.

The correspondence between Titian and the
King shows the painter in the least attractive light.
He was constantly asking for money, claiming,
often correctly, that he had not been paid for
previous work, that the annual pension of 200
scudi, bestowed upon him for life by Charles in
1548, had been withheld by the King's agents, and
that in his old age (which he exaggerated
deliberately) he had to live in misery and poverty.

Surprisingly little is known about Titian's
private life. Yet the image he presents of himself,
as an impoverished artist working solely for the
love of his patron, is clearly wrong. Not only had
he reached the unprecedented social status of a
nobleman, he was also a rich man.

It is obvious from his letters that Titian felt the

**A caricature of Titian**
*(right) Titian's life was full of financial battles, and he
was notoriously money-minded. A contemporary artist
Jacopo Bassano caricatured him as a moneylender.*

# Titian's Notorious Friend

Poet, playwright and scandalmonger, Pietro Aretino (1492-1556) was Titian's closest friend. The two men first met in Venice in 1527: two years previously, Aretino had been forced to leave Rome after writing a series of pornographic sonnets. Though these poems gained him notoriety, his lasting fame rests mainly on six volumes of letters – many of which were written to Titian.

Aretino delighted in gossip, satire, abuse, and even blackmail – a fact which earned him the nickname 'the scourge of princes'. But in Titian's case, he put his pen to a worthier cause – publicizing his friend's genius, and playing a crucial role in spreading his name and reputation throughout Europe.

Scala

**Pietro Aretino (1545)**
*(left) Although he was one of Titian's most ardent admirers, Aretino criticized this portrait of himself for its lack of finish.*

**Erotic poetry book**
*(below) In 1524 Aretino wrote a series of sexually explicit poems, accompanied by equally explicit engravings by Marcantonio Raimondi. They caused a storm of controversy in Rome, and the poet was forced to leave the Holy City.*

Pitti, Florence

Scala

freedom and its safety in the lagoon. Two of the arrivals were the poet Pietro Aretino and the sculptor and architect Jacopo Sansovino. Their close friendship with Titian was such that the Venetians referred to it as the triumvirate, with Titian and Aretino, in particular, exploiting their influence with their respective patrons to further each others interests.

Very little is known about Titian's last years. His eyesight was failing and his hand began to lose its control over the brush. The large workshop, led by Titian's talented son Orazio, was now mainly responsible for carrying out most of the work, with the master adding some final touches to paintings which were then passed off as by his own hand. King Philip remained the major recipient of these pictures, and there were no complaints about obvious workshop productions. As one Spanish nobleman told another in 1575: 'I believe that a blotch by Titian will be better than anything by another artist.'

In Venice new generations of painters had emerged, including Tintoretto and Veronese, with whom Titian and his workshop had to compete for local commissions. Yet none of them could aspire to his universal reputation, and when he died on 27 August 1576, during another outbreak of the plague, the painters of Venice planned to emulate the elaborate festivities with which the Florentines had buried Michelangelo in 1564. Yet the plague prohibited similarly lavish obsequies in honour of Titian, and he was quietly but ceremoniously interred in the church of Sta Maria dei Frari the day after he had died.

### Painting for a tomb
*(below) Titian began this magnificent* Pietà *in about 1575 with the intention that it should be placed above his own tomb. It was completed after his death by one of his many assistants.*

Accademia, Venice

# Living Paint

**In his long career, Titian was unsurpassed in his field. He brought to new heights the traditional Venetian love of sensuous colour and evolved a revolutionary style of expressive brushwork.**

'It is easy to see the haste with which it has been painted, and if there had been more time I would have had him do it over again.' This was Philip II's immediate comment on his *Portrait in Armour* of 1550/51 (p.135). Dissatisfied, he gave it to his aunt, Mary of Hungary. It took time for him to get used to, and admire, Titian's open brushwork, his loose handling of forms and colours. His aunt was more perceptive. When lending this portrait to Queen Mary of England, who was about to marry Philip, she wrote that the picture, like all others by Titian, had to be viewed from a distance.

## BOLD BRUSHWORK

Giorgio Vasari, having visited the artist in 1566, commented similarly on Titian's technique. His early works, Vasari said, had been executed with fineness and an unbelievable diligence, while 'these last pictures are executed with broad and bold strokes and smudges, so that from nearby nothing can be seen whereas from a distance they seem perfect.'

Vasari, himself an accomplished artist, realized

that this technique which gave to Titian's painting an appearance of spontaneous facility and ease, involved long and hard work: 'It is known that these works are much revised and that he went over them so many times with his colours that one can appreciate how much labour is involved.'

Palma Giovane, one of Titian's last assistants, has left us with a vivid description of his master's working methods. Titian used to sketch in his pictures with large masses of colour which formed the foundation of the composition. He would then turn them to the wall and leave them there, sometimes for several months, without looking at them. Returning to his picture, over long intervals, he would then build up his figures, correct and revise them and make any changes he felt necessary. Finally he would retouch the work, moderate the highlights by rubbing them with his fingers and harmonize the colours and tones; or he would, again with his fingers, add dark strokes or bright red spots to liven up the composition. According to Palma, in these last stages Titian painted more with his fingers than his brushes.

Somewhat grudgingly, Vasari admitted that

**The Andrians (1523-5)**
*(above) This is one of several large mythologies commissioned by Alfonso d'Este for his new study. Titian was anxious to better the work of his old master, Giovanni Bellini, who had also contributed to the scheme.*

**A rare drawing**
*(far left) Titian seems to have made comparatively few drawings. Surprisingly, however, several elaborate preparatory studies exist for his destroyed masterpiece* The Battle of Spoleto.

**Ranuccio Farnese (1542)**
*(left) Titian painted superb portraits throughout his career for a string of aristocratic patrons.*

Staatliche Graphische Sammlung, Munich

National Gallery of Art, Washington D.C.

Prado, Madrid  Scala

Pitti Gallery, Florence

**The Entombment (1559)**
*(below) The vivid, saturated colours of this religious work – with its glowing reds, blues and golds – are a feature of Titian's late style.*

**St Mary Magdalen (c.1535)**
*(above) Popular inventions, like this incredibly sensual interpretation of a devotional theme, were copied and churned out by Titian's busy studio.*

this technique produced 'judicious, beautiful and stupendous' results. As a Florentine, he believed that the proper way to go about painting was to start with sketches on paper, to work out every detail of a composition in carefully studied drawings. The final drawing could then be transferred almost mechanically to the panel or canvas, and coloured in. This was the method by which the masterpieces of Florentine art, of Leonardo, Raphael and, above all, Michelangelo had been achieved. While Vasari admired the colours of the Venetian painters, he deplored their neglect of drawing – for him the most fundamental part of painting.

In Rome in 1545, Vasari introduced Michelangelo to Titian who was working on a picture of *Danaë*. The visitors praised Titian's work, as was only polite, yet after they had left him Michelangelo told Vasari 'that Titian's colouring and his style much pleased him, but that it was a pity that in Venice men did not learn to draw well from the beginning, and that those painters did not pursue a better method in their studies.'

This was not simply a matter of professional jealousy or competition between Michelangelo and Titian, although that was also part of the argument. The two masters pursued almost totally different aims in their painting. Michelangelo

Prado, Madrid  AISA

**Vigorous draughtsmanship**
*This powerful drawing may have been a study for*
Tarquin and Lucretia. *X-rays show that the painting*
*(right) was originally similar in composition.*

## TRADEMARKS
# Free Brushwork

Titian's brushwork has a beauty of its own, irrespective of what it represents. He was the first artist to realize the potential of oil paint, with all its richness and variety of texture.

**Tarquin and Lucretia (c.1571)**
*(above and detail right)*
*This late masterpiece shows the astonishing energy of Titian's style even when he was in his 80s. It depicts a scene from the legendary early history of Rome – the virtuous Lucretia was raped by Tarquin, son of a tyrant, and in anguish killed herself the following day. Tarquin was later exiled and slain. Titian conveys the drama of the tragic story with breathtaking vigour, the bold brushwork helping to suggest the violent movement. Lucretia's expression evokes her terror and despair.*

concentrated on the nude male figure as an heroic ideal with expressive and dramatic movements. Titian's paintings, according to his friend Ludovico Dolce, depicted the whole visual world with all its various aspects and different effects. The delicacy of the female form, the softness of flesh, the moisture in the eyes of St Mary Magdalen (p.115) or Lucretia (p.117) – these were qualities which Michelangelo with all his mastery of drawing could not capture in his works. Watching the sun set beyond the Grand Canal, Aretino was reminded of Titian's art and exclaimed 'Oh Titian, where are you now?'; no drawing could convey the effects of light he conjured up in his paintings.

Since his early days, when he had been working with Giorgione, Titian had tried to convey in his pictures an overall sense of mood, of atmosphere: the tranquillity of pastoral landscapes, or the buoyancy of drinking and dancing in *The Andrians* (p.114), the heavenly glow of *The Assumption* (p.124) or the murderous drama of the *St Peter Martyr* (p.111). These are all effects which depend on an overall impression, not on the detailed study of particular features. Titian's late

style, often and anachronistically described as 'impressionistic' by modern critics, enforces the overall effect he is aiming at: the spectator has to stand back and take in the whole of the composition. If he gets too close to the painted surface, the picture will dissolve in blots and smudges.

A late work like the *Pietà* (p.113) which was completed after Titian's death, shows all the means which the artist employed to achieve such an overall effect, in this case that of a tragic, gloomy night scene: broad strokes with a heavily loaded brush mark out the individual figures which seem to vibrate in the flickering torchlight.

### WORKSHOP PRODUCTIONS

Titian's technique of painting had one further advantage which must have appealed to his economical mind. The intermediate stages of execution, between the initial, inventive sketch and the final retouching, could often be left to assistants. From the 1540s, Titian seems to have employed a large workshop (although probably

# The Loves of Jupiter

The works of the Roman poet Ovid were extremely popular during the Renaissance and provided a rich fund of inspiration for artists of all kinds. Indeed, his *Metamorphoses*, which recounted stories depicting the transformations that abounded in ancient legend, did more than any other work of literature to transmit to posterity the imaginative beauties of Greek mythology. Jupiter – the supreme god of the Romans – figures prominently in the *Metamorphoses*, as he often disguised himself in various forms in the course of his amorous adventures. Paintings of such subjects appealed greatly to the sophisticated private collectors who began to rival the church as patrons in the 16th century.

**Correggio** (c.1494-1534) **Jupiter and Io**
*Jupiter changed himself into a cloud to visit the beautiful Io, trying to hide his infidelity from his wife, Juno. Correggio's erotic masterpiece was painted for Federico Gonzaga, Duke of Mantua, and was later owned by Charles V.*

**Paolo Veronese** (1528-88) **The Rape of Europa**
*Veronese was one of the leading Venetian artists in the generation after Titian's death. His painting makes a splendid pageant of the theme, whereas Titian (p.131) emphasized its dramatic energy.*

Ducal Palace, Venice

Kunsthistorisches Museum, Vienna

not as large as Raphael's earlier in the century, or Rubens' in the next one). At least 30 of his assistants are recorded by name. Very few of them, perhaps only Tintoretto and El Greco, went on to become great artists in their own right. Most of them, like Titian's son Orazio, his cousin Marco, or Girolamo Dente (who stayed with Titian for 30 years) became totally absorbed in the workshop.

To commission a work by Titian could often mean paying for a workshop production. This was an old Venetian tradition. The earlier workshops of the Bellinis and Vivarinis had operated in much the same way. Yet Titian's own technique seems to have undermined the old system: patrons and critics expected to find his genius expressed in every single brushstroke, and they were often not happy with the way in which assistants did the major work for him 'which he then finishes with two strokes of his brush and sells as his own work.' As Palma Giovane confirms, true lovers of art had caught on to the new notion of the individual 'divine genius', whose work, even if unfinished and sketchy, was more valuable than the polished product of an anonymous workshop.

# Sacred and Profane Love

In c.1514 Niccolò Aurelio, one of Venice's most senior civil servants, commissioned the so-called *Sacred and Profane Love*. As far as its subject-matter is concerned, this beautiful picture remains an enigma. Various interpretations have been put forward, of which the most popular maintains that the painting is an allegory of earthly and spiritual love, showing the terrestrial and celestial Venuses. However, there could be a much less esoteric explanation: Niccolò Aurelio married in 1514 and may have commissioned this picture to celebrate the event. The woman dressed in white may be his bride, who is being gently initiated into the mysteries of love by the naked goddess Venus. Cupid, her companion, stirs the waters of the fountain, aiding his mistress in her amorous designs.

## Heraldic Clues

NICOLAVS AVRELIVS
MDXIIII. XXIII. AVGVS

Titian has included the family shield of Niccolò Aurelio in the frieze on the fountain (right), and the coat of arms of his bride, Laura Bagarotto, has recently been discovered in the silver dish above. This makes the 'marriage-picture' theory seem even more attractive.

**Bridal dress**
The woman clothed in white, the traditional colour of Venetian bridal gowns, wears myrtle in her hair – a plant which is sacred to Venus and symbolizes marriage.

Borghese Gallery, Rome

'Beauty Adorned and
Beauty Unadorned'

Francucci

Scala

**Idyllic setting**
*(above) The lovely
landscape in the
background conjures up the
beauty of the Veneto region
where Titian was born.*

**Classical sources**
*(left) Titian based the horse
in the fountain frieze
(below) on the famous
bronze horses of San Marco
in Venice.*

**Flora (c.1520)**
*(right) This portrait
represents the same ideal of
beauty as the two women in*
Sacred and Profane
Love.

Scala

Uffizi, Florence

**Obscure symbolism**
*(left) The meaning of the
mysterious frieze on the
fountain is still unclear.
One theory suggests that it
shows the taming of animal
passion – symbolized by the
restraining of an unbridled
horse. On the other hand,
the relief may have some
private significance of an
erotic nature for the patron.*

# Gallery

The early works of Titian, like the Noli Me Tangere, reveal the influence of Giorgione – in the graceful elongation of the figures and the pastoral landscape – although the dramatic intensity of the gestures already heralds Titian's mature style. In The Assumption of the Virgin, the vigorous poses and spectacular colouring reveal the hallmarks of Titian's

**Noli Me Tangere** *c.1508*
43″ × 35¾″ National
Gallery, London

*This early painting tells the story of Christ's appearance to the Magdalen, after the Resurrection. According to the gospel of St John, the Magdalen, who was weeping over the empty tomb, at first mistook him for a gardener. When she recognized Christ she reached out to touch him, but he gently bade her 'touch me not' ('noli me tangere'). Titian shows the graceful figure of Christ holding a gardener's hoe and drawing his robes back from the outstretched hand of the kneeling Magdalen.*

individual genius. But it was with his portraits, rather than his Venetian altarpieces, that Titian attracted the attention of some of the most important and influential men in Europe. The Man with a Blue Sleeve and The Young Englishman are two of his masterpieces.

For the Duke of Ferrara he painted recreations of classical works of art, including the boisterous Bacchus and Ariadne, while the famous Venus of Urbino was acquired by the future Duke of Urbino. Titian's most powerful patrons were the Emperor Charles V and his son, Philip II of Spain. For Charles he painted portraits and religious works, including a striking equestrian portrait, and for his son he executed a series of dazzling mythologies.

**The Man with a Blue Sleeve** *c.1511*
31¾″ × 26″ National Gallery, London

*This half-length portrait, traditionally thought to be of the poet Ariosto, may, in fact, be a self-portrait. The sitter is shown against a plain background, leaning against a parapet on which Titian has inscribed his own initials. His wonderfully self-assured pose and confident gaze are almost as striking as the beautifully painted blue sleeve which, in a brilliant show of illusionism, seems to project out of the picture space.*

Scala

**Sacred and Profane Love** *c.1514*
46½″ × 109¾″ Borghese Gallery, Rome

*Titian painted this hauntingly beautiful picture for Niccolò-Aurelio,
secretary to the Council of Ten. Its meaning is obscure and the title,
'Sacred and Profane Love', is an 18th-century concoction. Only two
figures can be identified with any certainty: the draped nude is Venus
and the little boy is Cupid. The sumptuously dressed woman, who
seems oblivious of the goddess's presence, may be a mortal woman who
sits at the Fountain of Venus, reflecting on the nature of love.*

**The Assumption of the
Virgin** *1516-18*
271½″ × 141¾″ Santa
Maria dei Frari, Venice

*Titian painted this great
altarpiece for the church of
Santa Maria dei Frari,
one of the most important
churches in Venice. The
Madonna ascends to
heaven in a golden halo of
light, watched by the
astonished Apostles
beneath her. The dramatic
intensity of the scene is
heightened by Titian's
glorious use of colour. The
red robes of the two
Apostles, who anchor the
composition, are echoed in
the crimson gown of the
Madonna and in the cloak
of God the Father above
her, giving an upward
thrust to the whole
composition.*

**Bacchus and Ariadne** *c.1520-23*
68¾″ × 74¾″ National Gallery, London

*This exuberant scene, painted for Alfonso d'Este, shows the wine-god
Bacchus and his carousing followers coming across Ariadne, the
daughter of King Minos of Crete, who has been abandoned by her lover
Theseus. Titian based his account on details from Ovid and Catullus,
and included the two cheetahs from Alfonso's private zoo.*

### Venus of Urbino *1538*
46¾" × 65" Uffizi, Florence

*Although this famous painting is known as the
'Venus of Urbino', it was never in Urbino and
possibly does not even represent the classical goddess
of love. The painting may simply show a beautiful
woman in her boudoir – a sort of Renaissance
'pin-up'. Indeed, Guidobaldo II, who acquired the
picture, referred to it merely as 'the naked woman'.
Titian was an intimate of Pietro Aretino's at this
time, and shared his friend's dislike for 'anything that
savours of pedantry'. His 'Venus' is shown in an
antique pose – with her hand in a traditional position
of modesty – but she gazes quietly and seductively at
the onlooker, in a spirit of shared intimacy.*

Scala

**The Young Englishman** *c.1540-45*
43¾" × 36½" Pitti Gallery, Florence

*During his lifetime, Titian established a reputation as Europe's
supreme portraitist. The so-called 'Young Englishman' – the sitter has
never been satisfactorily identified – is one of his most penetrating
character studies, focusing on the handsome aristocrat's impassive face
with its cool, piercing grey eyes.*

**Charles V on Horseback** *1548*
130¾″ × 109¾″ Prado, Madrid

*This splendid portrait, which celebrates Charles V's famous victory at
the Battle of Mühlberg, shows the Emperor in an equestrian pose which
dates back to the antique equestrian statue of Marcus Aurelius in
Rome. The marvellous landscape, bathed in the glow of sunset, reveals
why Titian was renowned for his ability to paint natural effects.*

Joseph S. Martin/Artothek

**Danaë** *c.1549-50*
50¾" × 85½" Prado, Madrid

*Between c.1554 and 1562 Titian painted six mythological canvases for*
*Philip II of Spain, which he called his 'poesie' – paintings which are*
*based on poetical texts, notably Ovid's* Metamorphoses. *At one time,*
*he considered including this erotic scene – in which Jupiter seduces*
*Danaë in the form of a shower of gold – in the series.*

**The Rape of Europa** *1559-62*
70″ × 80¾″ Isabella Stewart Gardner Museum, Boston

*In this, the last of the 'poesie', Titian shows the rape of Europa by the insatiable Jupiter, now in the guise of a bull. A winged infant ('putto') cheekily pursues the couple on the back of a dolphin, while Europa's companions watch helplessly from the shore. The vivid colouring and bold brushwork are typical of Titian's late style.*

# The Holy Roman Emperor

**Charles V inherited a vast multinational empire, and had to spend most of his life fighting to hold it together. Exhausted and overstrained, he at last gave up his throne.**

As the most powerful ruler of his time, Charles V was able to ensure that posterity would see him through the eyes of the greatest portrait painter. He patronized, flattered and ennobled Titian and, in return, the Venetian artist created the most enduring and convincing images of the Emperor's life – from young manhood to premature old age. These works form a moving record of the price paid for greatness or, at least, greatness under relentless pressure.

## THE YOUNG EMPEROR

Charles had greatness thrust upon him. Thanks to two generations of dynastic marriages arranged by his grandfather, the Holy Roman Emperor Maximilian, Charles became a power in Europe before he was out of his teens. He was born on 24 February 1500 at Ghent, in the dominions of his father, Philip, Duke of Burgundy. When Philip died in 1506, Charles inherited the Burgundian lands – most of the Low Countries, plus strategically important territories on both sides of France's eastern border. When his maternal grandfather, Ferdinand, died in 1516, Charles became King of Spain, southern Italy, Sicily, Sardinia, and most of the new-found Americas. And when Maximilian died, Charles inherited the title 'King of Germany', together with control of Austria and other lands in south-eastern Europe. The chance was also created to take Maximilian's place as head of the Holy Roman Empire.

The Empire was a curious survival from an earlier age. It began in the 9th century when the Frankish King Charlemagne conquered most of Europe and had himself crowned by the Pope as the recognized successor to the Roman Emperors in the West (hence the 'Holy' and 'Roman'). On his death, Charlemagne's sons divided his possessions between them, and the Empire was eventually restricted to the mainly German-speaking lands of Central Europe.

But whereas England, France and Spain gradually developed into centralized nation states, the Holy Roman Empire remained feudal in structure. The Emperor exercised little real control,

*Mauro Pucciarelli*

Palazzo Vecchio, Florence

**The coronation**
*(above) By 1530, Charles V had gained control in Italy and could insist on a second coronation by the Pope himself.*

**The lonely emperor**
*(right) This compassionate portrait of Charles V, painted by Titian in 1548, reveals the loneliness of Europe's most powerful man.*

*Joachim Blauel/Artothek*

**The capture of Tunis**
*(right) A brilliant campaign against the Arab corsairs in North Africa in 1535 finally established Charles' power and authority in Europe. For decades, the corsairs had been gaining in power and posed an increasing threat to ships plying the western Mediterranean, but Charles' splendid fleet succeeded in driving them from Tunis and putting their leader Barbarossa ('Redbeard') to flight.*

Mauro Pucciarelli

and it was his more powerful vassals – such as the provinces of Saxony, Bavaria and Brandenburg – who built up effective governments and armies in their own territories. By the 16th century, the Empire had become a loose confederation of several hundred more or less autonomous units, ranging from formidable states to tiny fiefs.

All attempts to increase the effective power of the Emperor had failed, yet the imperial office retained its glamour. In some sense the Emperor was still regarded as the head of western Christendom. Charles was not the only notable who thought the Imperial throne worth having: Francis I of France became a candidate, and even Henry VIII of England considered standing. The Emperor did not inherit his title but was elected. However, since 1438 the title had, in fact, always been held by one of Charles's family, the Habsburgs, whose Austrian territories gave them a power base within the Empire.

In 1519 the seven Electors unanimously chose Charles as the new Holy Roman Emperor though this satisfactory result cost him a crippling 850,000 florins in bribes. Charles may have believed that he could decisively strengthen Imperial authority. But in practice the sheer extent of his dominions proved a liability. Given the slowness of 16th-century communications, the Habsburg empire was impossibly unwieldy. The only unifying factor

Edistudio

Bulloz

**The Empress Isabella**
*(above) Charles V never really recovered from the death of his wife in 1539. He asked Titian to paint this portrait of her in 1545.*

**Charles V's shield**
*(left) Charles' reign was a time of almost continuous warring and his reputation is founded as much on his exploits in the field of battle as upon his statesmanship.*

### Abdication

*(right) In a touching ceremony in Brussels, the exhausted Emperor completed the first step of his abdication in October 1555, handing over the Netherlands to Philip.*

was Charles himself, and he could not be everywhere. As a soldier he had a good many successes, but with enemies on so many fronts – French, Turks, German princes, the popes – he was rarely able to exploit his victories to the full. Travelling incessantly, fighting one war after another and emptying his treasury, he managed – just – to hold on. His larger aims – to strengthen the empire, defeat the infidel, crush the heretic – remained unachieved.

The most implacable of Charles' enemies were the French, who saw themselves encircled by Habsburg power all the way from the Pyrenees to Flanders. Their attempts to break out led to a series of Italian wars that kept Charles busy until 1528. This was probably the most successful period of his reign. In 1525 Francis I was decisively beaten and taken prisoner at Pavia and, although the French king went back on his promises as soon as he was released, the imperialists kept the advantage. Charles captured Milan and – with Genoa, Florence and the Papacy as satellites – Italy was brought firmly into the Habsburg camp.

Although Charles was a staunch Catholic, Pope Clement VII had been hostile to him for political reasons. In 1527 imperial troops – many of them Protestant mercenaries – descended on Rome, sacked the city and made the Pope a prisoner.

Palais Granvelle, Bescançon

### The monastery at Yuste

*(above) Putting the cares of the empire behind him, Charles lived out the last months of his life in peace in a house attached to the monastery at Yuste in Spain.*

After this experience, Clement 'resolved to live and die an imperialist'. In 1530 he was reconciled with Charles at Bologna, where the Emperor also had his first meeting with Titian. The painter's first commissioned portrait of the Emperor, however, was not done from life, but from an earlier oil by the Austrian court painter Jacob Seisinegger. Even so, the flat rendition of Seisinegger was transformed into a compassionate study of an already lonely man.

## ATTACKED FROM ALL SIDES

Outside Italy, the French wars carried on into the 1530s and 40s, and the unscrupulous Francis I even went as far as to ally himself with the Ottoman Turks. The Ottoman Empire reached the peak of power and ambition under Suleiman I, battering at the gates of Vienna in the east while Muslim corsairs penetrated the western Mediterranean. Charles counter-attacked in North Africa, capturing Tunis in 1535 but failing disastrously to take Algiers in 1541.

Inevitably, with all these distractions, Charles did little to strengthen the imperial power in Germany or check a new source of dissension – Protestantism. The Protestant Reformation had begun only three years before Charles became Emperor, and one of his first acts was to assemble the imperial parliament – known as the Diet –

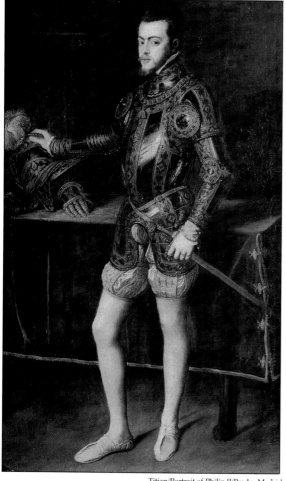

### Philip II and the Armada

*(left and above) When Charles V handed the crown of Spain to his son Philip, Spain was the most powerful country in Europe, but England proved to be a constant thorn in Philip's side. In 1588, he sent a great armada to invade England, but the lumbering Spanish fleet was put to flight.*

which condemned the new doctrine.

But, by the time peace with the French and Turks gave him some freedom of action, Lutheranism had found influential supporters among the princes. Charles nevertheless took the field. At Mühlberg he won one of his greatest victories – a victory that Titian was summoned to immortalize in *Portrait of Charles V on Horseback* painted at Augsburg in January 1548. In Titian's epic painting, the monarch wears the very armour in which he won the battle. His black steed canters across a now tranquil landscape. It set the style for the princely portraiture of the era.

Like so many of Charles's triumphs, however, the lull brought by Mühlberg was short-lived. Alarmed by his increased power, the Protestant princes leagued themselves with the French and, after a long struggle, the Peace of Augsburg (1555) left the Empire weak and Lutheranism unbroken.

Shortly afterwards, Charles abdicated. His empire, clearly too great for one man, was divided between his brother Ferdinand, who took over Austria and the Crown of the Empire, and his son Philip, who received all the rest. Charles, who had grown to love Spain, retired to a villa attached to a monastery at Yuste in Estramadura. He took with him Titian's huge altarpiece *La Gloria*, in which he and his son appear paying homage. Charles lived at Yuste in pious comfort, reading, over-eating and listening to divine service, until his death on 21 September 1558.

Charles' son Philip became an even more lavish patron of Titian and even more thoroughly Spanish, ruling his empire from Madrid. The Dutch revolted against him and the English defeated his Armada but, under Philip, Spain enjoyed its 'Golden Age'. As for the tenacious Habsburgs, they ruled in Spain until 1700, remained Holy Roman Emperors until 1806, and ruled a sprawling, multinational Austrian Empire, until a World War destroyed it in 1918.

### The monastery at Escorial

*(left) As a memorial to his father Charles V, Philip had the vast monastery of San Lorenzo built near Madrid. It contains the tombs of nearly all subsequent Spanish kings.*

# A Year in the Life 1572

**In the Spring, a band of Protestant 'Sea Beggars' challenged the might of Titian's patron – Philip II of Spain – and triggered a string of uprisings throughout the Spanish-controlled Netherlands. The bloody conflict between Catholic and Protestant continued unabated – culminating in the massacre of thousands.**

In the early 1570s, the Netherlands (roughly modern Belgium and Holland) were ruled with an iron fist by the Spanish governor, the Duke of Alva. Spaniards held all positions of power, and thousands of dissidents and Protestants were hanged or burned. Alva's leading opponent, William the Silent, Prince of Orange, had been defeated and exiled, and the only men in arms against the regime were the Sea Beggars, a motley band of Protestant sea-raiders. Although the Netherlands seethed with resentment, Alva and Philip II of Spain, Titian's royal patron, believed they held complete control.

Then, on 1 April 1572, 25 of the Sea Beggars' storm-battered ships put into the port of Brill, found the Spanish garrison absent, and took over the town. They followed up this lucky success by seizing another port, Flushing, and this fired the

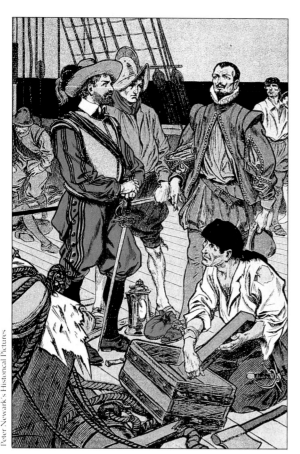

*Peter Newark's Historical Pictures*

**William of Orange**
*(right) William the Silent, Prince of Orange (1533-1584), led an invasion of the Netherlands in 1572 with an army assembled in Germany. He hoped to repel the forces of Philip II of Spain. In gratitude for his efforts the people of Holland and Zeeland elected him Stadtholder or governor.*

**St Bartholomew's Day massacre**
*At dawn on Sunday 24 August 1572, there began an attempt by Charles IX and his mother Catherine de' Medici to purge France of its protestant Huguenot population. The massacre spread from Paris and up to 50,000 people were murdered in the following months.*

*Jean-Loup Charmet*

**Drake on the Spanish Main**
*(above) In 1572 Francis Drake (c.1543-1596) successfully attacked the Spanish stronghold of Nombre de Dios, Panama.*

**Tycho Brahe's universe**
*(right) On 11 November 1572, Tycho Brahe, a Danish astronomer, first measured the position of a brilliant star now called 'Tycho's supernova'. His measurements altered contemporary concepts of the universe.*

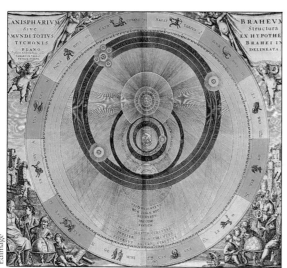

*Edimage*

Tycho Brahe's Planisphere

*Mauro Pucciarelli*

136

landsmen to act. Spontaneously, the citizens of one town after another – Rotterdam, Gouda, Haarlem, Leyden, Delft – rose against the Spaniards and, in July, William the Silent arrived to lead the revolt. The Netherlands were ablaze, and Alva's savage reaction – burning, sacking and indiscriminate killing – only stiffened resistance.

## THE LONG STRUGGLE

The struggle was to continue for almost forty years, draining Spanish resources and bogging down her armies. In the event, the Spaniards held on to the southern Netherlands, which therefore remained Catholic, while the north became Protestant and independent.

Spain might have lost the entire Netherlands if the French had intervened on the side of the rebels. But France was deeply divided between Catholics and Protestants (Huguenots). To complicate matters, the King, Charles IX, was weak. His mother, the able, unscrupulous Catherine de' Medici, dominated him and struggled to preserve the independence of the Crown against rival Catholic and Protestant factions. It was not an easy task.

When the Huguenot leader, Admiral Coligny, began to influence her son, Catherine decided to eliminate him. The subsequent assassination attempt went wrong (Coligny was only wounded) and Catherine, faced with exposure, tried to make Charles himself agree to her plans. The unstable young King finally gave way but cried: 'Very well! But kill them all, so

### Ben Jonson
*(left) Ben Jonson the playwright was born in 1572, and died in 1637. He was the author of the supreme dramatisation of Elizabethan low-life –* Bartholomew Fair *– and of* Volpone, or the Fox, *a biting satire.*

### A plot discovered
*(right) In 1572 both houses of parliament demanded the execution of Mary Stuart for her part in a plot to utilise the forces of Catholic Spain to wrest the throne from Elizabeth.*

### John Knox
*(below) John Knox, leader of the Scottish Reformation, died in November 1572. This painting shows him at one of his audiences with Mary Queen of Scots who was to become his enemy.*

François Dubois/St. Bartholomew's Day Massacre/Musée, Lausanne

Samuel Sidley/Mary, Queen of Scots and John Knox (detail)/Towneley Hall Art Gallery, Burnley

that not one will be left to reproach me afterwards!' And so Catherine's coolly premeditated political murder turned into a sectarian massacre.

## THE MASSACRE BEGINS

In the early hours of Sunday 24 August – St Bartholomew's Day – armed men entered Coligny's house and stabbed him to death. At four o'clock in the morning, the agreed signal for the general attack rang out. Specially armed groups began the killing, working from prepared lists of important Huguenots. But the slaughter soon become more general as the Catholic populace joined in. Thousands of Protestant men, women and children were done to death.

Philip, like most Catholics, was overjoyed; he even violated the sombre protocol of his own court by laughing out loud. The Senate of Titian's native Venice sent the French King their congratulations. And in Rome, the new Pope, Gregory XIII, celebrated with bonfires, had medals struck and commissioned a mural showing the massacre.

The celebrations turned out to be premature. The Huguenots barricaded themselves in their strongholds, and in the winter of 1572-73 the chief of these – the town of La Rochelle – successfully withstood a long siege. Within a few months new political alignments restored the state of truce, leaving the situation much as it had existed before the massacre. The bloodshed had achieved nothing except the needless slaughter of countless innocents.

Scala

State Archive, Siena

**Pope Gregory's calendar**
*(left) In 1572, Pope Pius V was succeeded by Ugo Boncampagni – Pope Gregory XIII – who held office for the next 13 years. With the help of the Jesuit mathematician, Christopher Clavius (1537-1612), he brought about necessary calendar reform to rectify the inaccuracy of the Julian calendar. It is the Gregorian model that we use today.*

**Battle for the Netherlands**
*(right) This print depicts one of the many battles which raged off the coast of the Netherlands between the indigenous Protestants and the brutal forces of Catholic Spanish occupation under the Duke of Alva. On 1 April 1572 a party of Sea Beggars – a piratical anti-Catholic liberating force – succeeded in taking Brill. Other ports followed, and the stern grip of Spanish despotism was progressively weakened.*

Jean-Loup Charmet

# GALLERY GUIDE

### Leonardo da Vinci
*The Annunciation* (pp.20-21), is in Florence (Uffizi Gallery). The c.1483 version of *The Virgin of the Rocks* (p.27) is in Paris (Louvre) and the c.1506 version (p.32) is in London (National Gallery). Visitors to these galleries can also compare two versions of the *Virgin and Child with St Anne*. The fresco of *The Last Supper* (pp.24-5) – now restored – is in the Refectory of Santa Maria delle Grazie, Milan. His *Adoration of the Magi* is in Florence (Uffizi). Of the portraits, *Ginevra de' Benci* (p.22) can be seen in Washington DC (National Gallery of Art) and the *Mona Lisa* is in the Louvre, Paris. The major collection of Leonardo's drawings is held in the Royal Collection, Windsor.

### Michelangelo
The marble *Bacchus* (Bargello, Florence) is Michelangelo's first major work, but his *David* (p.55) (Accademia, Florence) established him as a genius. Of his Madonnas, the *Madonna and Child* is in the Church of Onze Lieve Vrouwe, Bruges. The unfinished marble of *St Matthew*, (Accademia, Florence) originally intended for the *Tomb of Julius* (p.47), was influenced by the Laöcoon group (p.46). Two other sculptures (now in the Louvre) originally intended for the revised plan of Julius's tomb, are the unfinished *Struggling Captive*, and the *Dying Captive*, both c.1513.

### Raphael
The early *Betrothal of the Virgin* (p.86) is in the Brera Academy, Milan. Raphael's *Madonna del Cardellino* is in Florence (Uffizi) and *The Madonna of the Field* is in Vienna (Kunsthistorisches Museum). His famous drawn self-portrait as a boy of 16 (p.76), is now in Oxford, England, and another (p.75) – painted when he was about 23 – is in the Uffizi.

Other portraits are the bearded *Baldassare Castiglione* (p.78) (Louvre, Paris) and *Maddalena Doni* (Pitti, Florence). Raphael's *Giuliano de' Medici* is missing, but there is a copy in New York (The Metropolitan Museum). The *Canigiani Holy Family* (Munich Art Gallery) is an example of Raphael's mastery of pyramidal construction, which he learned from Leonardo.

### Titian
*The Flight into Egypt* is in Leningrad (Hermitage), while the *Pastoral Concert* is in Paris (Louvre). *The Madonna and Child with SS Anthony of Padua and Roch* is held in the Prado, Madrid, and the *Gypsy Madonna* in the Kunsthistoriches Museum, Vienna. The festive *Bacchanal* (Prado, Madrid) is part of a series with *The Worship of Venus* in the same gallery. The *Assumption of the Virgin* (p.124) altarpiece for the Church of Santa Maria dei Frari was the work that convinced art connoisseurs that Venice could rival the school of Rome. The Louvre in Paris has the *Madonna of the Rabbit*. The *Venus of Urbino* (pp.126-7) is in Florence (Uffizi) and another reclining nude, Titian's *Danäe*, is in the Galleria Nazionale, Naples. Of the portraits, the *Man with a Glove* and one of several *Portrait of a Man* canvases, are both in Paris (Louvre). *Portrait of a Gentleman* is in the Pitti Palace, Florence. Of the later portraits, Washington's National Gallery of Art has the young *Ranuccio Farnese* (p.114).

# BIBLIOGRAPHY

B. Berenson, *Italian Painters of the Renaissance*, Cornell University Press, Ithaca, 1980

K. Clark, *Leonardo da Vinci* (the complete paintings of Leonardo da Vinci with an introduction by L. D. Ettlinger), Weidenfeld & Nicholson, London, 1967

Kenneth Clark, *The Nude*, Princeton University Press, Princeton, 1972

L. Goldscheider, *Michelangelo: Paintings, Sculptures, Architecture*, Phaidon, Oxford, 1967

F. Hartt, *History of Italian Renaissance Art (Painting, Sculpture, Architecture)*, Abrams, New York, 1980

F. Hartt, *Michelangelo*, Abrams, New York, 1984

L. H. Heydenreich, *Leonardo da Vinci* (2 vols), Macmillan, London, 1954

L. Murray, *Michelangelo*, Oxford University Press, Oxford, 1980

W. Pater, *The Renaissance* (originally written and printed in *Fortnightly Review*, 1869), Academy, Chicago, 1977

A. E. Popham, *The Drawings of Leonardo da Vinci*, Merrimack Publishers Circle, Salem, 1981

W. E. Suida, *Raphael: Paintings and Drawings*, Phaidon, Oxford, 1942

G. Vasari, *The Lives of the Artists*, trans. G. Bull, Penguin, New York, 1966

H. E. Wethey, *The Paintings of Titian*, Phaidon, Oxford, 1970

H. Wölfflin, *Classic Art: An Introduction to the Italian Renaissance*, Cornell University Press, Ithaca, 1980

### The Bellini family

The Bellini family of Venice boasted three painters: Jacopo (c.1400-70/1), and his sons Gentile (c.1429/30-1507) and Giovanni (c.1430-1516). Only four pictures can be definitely attributed to Jacopo, as well as his two sketchbooks, which were used as a source of ideas by his sons. Although Gentile was ennobled by the Emperor for his work in 1469, it was Giovanni – usually accepted as the younger son – who made the greatest mark on 15th century painting. He influenced some of the leading artists of his own and the next generation: Giorgione and Titian, for example, studied under him. Himself influenced by Antonello, Giovanni became the greatest Venetian Madonna painter, and produced a succession of highly imaginative altarpieces, devotional works, and official commissions, such as the Doge Loredano (National Gallery, London).

Giovanni was also the first Venetian to use the new technique of mixing paints with oil, instead of egg as in tempera, and pioneered the use of landscape as a setting in which his figures moved or sat, rather than simply as a background to a picture, as in his St Jerome (1513, Sante Giovanni Crisostomo).

Some Giovanni Bellini paintings of note are: The Transfiguration (Museo Correr, Venice); The Suffering Christ (Louvre, Paris); and the Pietà (Plazzo Communale, Rimini).

### Antonio Correggio (1489-1534)

Unusual among the great Renaissance painters in that most of his work was in the provincial town of Parma, whereas the others worked in the great cities of Rome, Florence and Venice. He was a pupil of Mantegna, whose influence is clearly seen in the perspective of Correggio's frescoes of The Assumption of the Virgin, within the cupola of the Cathedral, Parma. Seen from below, they give the illusion that the figures are actually flying in space. These and other frescoes in the Church of St Giovanni Evangelista look forward to the Baroque. The flamboyance of Correggio's style, in which figures sometimes burst into the picture, was not highly thought of in his own time (when a contained, pyramidal composition was the ideal). But he was later seen to be producing a style more than a century ahead of his period, as in Antiope (Louvre, Paris), and Jupiter and Io (Kunsthistorisches Museum, Vienna).

### Giorgione (1476/8-1510)

A pupil of Bellini, he was considered by Vasari (in his Lives of the Artists) to be one of the founders of modern art, alongside Leonardo da Vinci. What set Giorgione's work apart from his contemporaries was his particular gift for expressing mood, which was to him more important than portraying action. Although he was considered to be very influential, details of his career are somewhat vague. It is known that in 1508 he worked with Titian on the frescoes of the Fondaco dei Tedeschi in Venice, though only fragments of these remain. When he died of the plague, still in his early thirties, several pictures were completed by other artists, including Titian, and this has compounded the problem of authenticating Giorgione's work. Of the few pictures that can be attributed to him with any certainty, the best-known are: The Madonna and Child with Saints (San Liberale, Castelfranco); the Tempest (c.1505 Accademia, Venice) – the first landscape of mood in which the figures are incidental rather than central to the painting; and The Trial of Moses (Uffizi, Florence).

### El Greco (Domenikos Theotokopoulos Greco) (1541-1614)

Invariably known as El Greco, he was born in Crete, at that time a colony of the Venetian Empire. Byzantine art was predominant there and he moved to Italy to develop his talents, studying first in Venice under Titian and Tintoretto and later (c.1572) in Rome. Here, for reasons not entirely clear, he became persona non grata in artistic circles, so he moved to Toledo, Spain, where he lived out the rest of his life.

In 1577, he produced his first masterpiece: The Assumption of the Virgin (Art Institute of Chicago). From then on, his paintings began to show the characteristics which made him the supreme exponent of the Mannerist style: the elongated figures in landscapes suffused in a cold eerie light, and the use of rather citric yellows, greens, reds and greys. Infuzed by his religious passion, his work has an intensity and power which are uniquely his; an El Greco painting is unmistakable even to the most untrained eye.

Outstanding examples of his work are The Agony in the Garden (Toledo Museum of Art, Ohio) and the Opening of the Fifth Seal (Metropolitan Museum of Art, New York).

### Andrea Mantegna (1431-1506)

Arguably the greatest northern Italian painter of the 15th century, Mantegna was also an antiquarian and a scholar. Three characteristics distinguish his paintings. Firstly, his figures often had a sculptural quality, as in his Judith (National Gallery of Ireland, Dublin). Secondly, he was fascinated by the technical problems of perspective and of foreshortening figures – his most notable work in this respect being The Dead Christ, a strange painting discovered in his studio after his death. Thirdly, he often included a great deal of architectural detail, as in Lodovico Gonzaga and his Family (Camera degli Sposi, Mantua). In The Agony in the Garden, (c.1460, National Gallery, London) even the rocky promontory in the foreground and the distant hills have a stepped, architectural form that bears little relation to nature. While working at the Camera degli Sposi for the Gonzaga family, some time between 1465-74, he painted a remarkable ceiling that gives the illusion of opening to the sky, above an ornate balustrade over

**El Espolio (The Disrobing of Christ) 1577**
(above) *This painting is still in the sacristy, Toledo Cathedral, the position for which it was painted. The sacristy is the room where vestments are kept and where priests robe and disrobe, so the subject was appropriate. The figure of Christ is one of the noblest El Greco ever painted – his sublime expression recalls Byzantian icons, which the artist knew in his native Crete.*

*which lean several figures looking down, while foreshortened* putti *balance precariously on the inner rail and a heavy planter filled with flowers seems about to crash down from its equally insecure perch. This predated by a century the celebrated ceiling fresco by Paolo Veronese, in which figures also peer down from a balcony. However, in his later years, Mantegna's continuing preoccupation with architectural and sculptural form reduced his palette to dull monochromes and his figures have a lifeless, sculptural form, as in the* Judgement of Solomon *(Louvre, Paris).*

### Perugino (c.1445/50-1523)
*Thought to have been a pupil of Piero della Francesca, Perugino went to Florence at the beginning of the 1470s. There, at about the same time as Leonardo da Vinci, he worked for Verrocchio.*

*Among his early work is a series of panels depicting the miracles of St Bernardino, in which garlanded archways open out on to romantic landscapes and his characters epitomize all that is gentle and pure. Although he was eventually to settle in that most violent of cities, Perugia, no such violence is ever evident in Perugino's work.*

*In 1481 he was commissioned to work on the frescoes for the Sistine Chapel, along with Botticelli, and his* Christ giving the Keys to St Peter *is another apparently simple, yet brilliantly composed example of his great gift for spatial composition – that is, the ability to create a three-dimensional effect that heightens the impression of vitality. Other examples are the* Pietà *(Florence Academy); and his* St Sebastian. *This is centred in front of an archway spanning two ornate pillars, with a delicately executed landscape beyond.*

### Jacopo Tintoretto (1518-1594)
*Little is known of Tintoretto's earliest years, but he became the foremost Mannerist painter of the Venetian school. Mannerism primarily emphasizes the human figure, often depicted in unnatural, distorted forms as in his* The Liberation of Arsinoe *(Gallery, Dresden). It was Tintoretto's declared intention to combine the colour of Titian and the draughtsmanship of Michelangelo. In fact, he developed a distinctive style of his own which relied more on direct emotional impact than on attention to realistic detail – and he worked at great speed.*

*His first major work was* St Mark Freeing a Christian Slave 1548, *(Accademia, Venice). Further striking examples are* The Discovery of the Body of St Mark *(Brera, Milan) and the* Transport of the Body of St Mark *(Accademia, Venice). In the latter, the shadowy figures in the background contrast dramatically with the illuminated elongated body of the Saint as they bear him through the streets while a storm rages overhead.*

*Tintoretto's major project in Venice was the decoration of the Scuola de San Rocco and its neighbouring church, the work being carried out in several stages between 1564 and 1587. More than 50 paintings were involved, some very large-scale. They illustrated the life of Christ and the life of the Virgin, as well as scenes from the Passion – all giving witness to the artist's mastery of light and colour. To see his greatest achievements, one must visit Venice; but many galleries worldwide have an example of the work of this last great Venetian painter of the Renaissance.*

# INDEX

**Note** Page numbers in italic type refer to illustrations.

## A

Abdallah, Abu *42*
Adrian, Cardinal 38
Alexander VI, Pope 36-9, 40, *41*, 47, 78, 101
Alfonso, Duke of Bisceglie 37
Alva, Fernando Alvarez de Toledo, Duke of 136-8, *138*
Apollo Belvedere *102*
Aretino, Pietro 113, *113*, 116
Ariosto, Ludovico *121*
Armada, Spanish (1588) *135*
artist's status 8
*Assumption of the Virgin, The* (Titian) *109*, 110, 116, *124*
Augsburg, Peace of (1555) 135
Aurelio, Niccolò, Chancellor of Venice 110, 118, 122
Aurelius, Marcus (statue) *129*
Avignon, France 101

## B

*Bacchus and Ariadne* (Titian) 111, *125*
Bahamas 42
Bassano, Jacopo
    *Christ and the Money-Lenders* (detail) *112*
Bellini, Gentile 108
Bellini, Giovanni 85, 108-109, 110, 114
    *Doge Loredano 140*
    *Madonna of the Meadow 85*
    *Pietà 140*
    *St Jerome 140*
    *Suffering Christ, The 140*
    *Transfiguration, The 140*
Bellini, Jacopo *140*
Belvedere, The (Rome) 102
Bembo, Pietro 39, 112
Bernini, Gianlorenzo 68, 71
    *Baldacchino, The 71*
    *St Peter's Square 68, 69*
Bertoldo di Giovanni 44
Biondo, Flavio 102
Boleyn, Anne, Queen of England 74
Boncampagni, Ugo *see* Gregory XIII, Pope
Borgia family 36-9, 40-41
Borgia, Cesare 18, 36-9, 41, 104
Borgia, Juan 37-8
Borgia, Lucrezia 36-9
Borgia, Rodrigo *see* Alexander VI
Botticini, Francesco
    *Tobias and the Archangels* (detail) *12*
Brahe, Tycho 136
Bramante, Donato d'Angelo 33, 41, 47, 68-72, 80, 101-102
    *St Peter's Rome 68, 69, 70*
    *Tempietto, The 68*

Bramantino (Bartolomeo Suardi) 78
Brunelleschi, Filippo 102
Buonarotti, Michelangelo *see* Michelangelo Buonarotti
Byzantium (Istanbul) *105*

## C

Calvin, John *106*
Cambrai, League of 105, 106
Camerino (Italy) 38
Capitol, The (Rome) *49*
Caprese (Tuscany) 44
cartoons 26, 50, 66, 83, 84, 97
Castel Sant' Angelo (Rome) 48, *73*, 101
Castiglione, Baldassare *78*, 82, 85
Catanei, Vannozza dei 37
Catherine of Aragon, Queen of England 74, *104*, 106
Cavalieri, Thomas 48, *48*
Caxton, William 42
Chambord, château de 33
Charlemagne, Emperor 132
Charles V, Emperor (Charles I of Spain) 48, 69, 72-4, 110-12, 117, *129, 132-5*
Charles VIII, King of France 41, 46
Charles IX, King of France 136-7
Chaucer, Geoffrey 42
Church of England 106
Clavius, Christopher 138
Clement VII, Pope 48, 73-4, 134
Coligny, Admiral 137
Colonna family *36*
Colonna, Vittoria 49, *49*
Colosseum (Rome) 100
Columbus, Christopher 41-2
Constantine, Arch of *101*
Constantine the Great (Roman Emperor) 68, 69, *101*
contrapposto 52-3
Cook, Captain James 72
Correggio, Antonio
    *Antiope 140*
    *Assumption of the Virgin 140*
    *Jupiter and Io 117*

## D

D'Amboise, Charles 18-19
Da Montefeltro, Guidobaldo, Duke of Urbino 77, 82
Da Sangallo, Antonio 70, 71
Da Sangallo, Giuliano 69
Da Vinci, Leonardo *see* Leonardo da Vinci
*David* (Michelangelo) 46, 52, 54, 77
Dei Catanei, Vannozza 37
Del Conte, Jacopino
    *Portrait of Michelangelo 8, 43*
Della Porta, Giacomo 70, 71
Della Rovere, Guidobaldo II, Duke of Urbino 111, 127

D'Este, Alfonso I, Duke of Ferrara 37, *109*, 110-11, *114, 125*
D'Este, Beatrice 15
Di Credi, Lorenzo
    *Portrait of Verrocchio 14*
    *Disrobing of Christ, The* (El Greco) *141*
*Disputà, The* (Raphael) 84, *98*
Dolce, Ludovico 82, 116
Donatello 51, 52
    *St Mark 52*
Dossi, Dosso 39
    *Bacchanal 38-9*
Drake, Sir Francis 136
Dürer, Albrecht 105

## E

Elizabeth I, Queen of England 137
Erasmus, Desiderius 9, 105
    *Praise of Folly 104*
Escorial Palace, Madrid *135*

## F

Farnese, Cardinal Alessandro *111*
Farnese, Giulia *41*
Farnese, Palazzo 70
Ferdinand of Castile, King of Spain 42, 105-106
Ferrara (Italy) 15, 37, 39
Florence 13-14, *13*, 32, 40-41, 44, *44*, 46-7, *51*, 55, 73-4, 77, *77*
Fondaco dei Tedeschi (German trader's warehouse, Venice) 109
Fontana, Domenico 70
foreshortening 50, 64
Forum Romanum (Rome) *46-7, 100-101*
Fra Giocondo 69
Francis I, King of France 19, 72, 133, 134
fresco 52-3
Fulvio, Andrea 101
    *Antiquitaties Urbi 103*

## G

Gallerani, Cecilia *23*
Ghirlandaio, Domenico 44, 52
    *Birth of John the Baptist 44*
Giocondo, Fra 69
Giorgione da Castelfranco *109*, 110, 116, 140
    *frescoes 140*
    *Madonna and Child with Saints, The 140*
    *Tempest, The 110, 140*
    *Trial of Moses, The 140*
Giovane, Palma 114
Gonzaga, Elisabetta 78
Gonzaga, Federico II, Marquis of

Mantua *110,* 111, 117
Gonzaga, Francesco 38
Greco, El (Domenikos Theotokopoulus) 117
    *Agony in the Garden 140*
    *Assumption of the Virgin, The 140*
    *Disrobing of Christ, The 141*
    *Opening of the Fifth Seal 140*
Gregorian Calendar *138*
Gregory XIII, Pope 138, *138*
Guidobaldo II, Duke of Urbino 127
Guild of St Luke 12

## H

Habsburg family 133-4, 135
Hadrian, Emperor of Rome (bust) 101
Hawaii 72
Henry VIII, King of England 74, 104, *105,* 106, 133
Holy Roman Empire 132-5
Huguenots 36-8

## I

Inca Empire *72*
indulgences 68
Ingres, Jean-Auguste-Dominique
    *Death of Leonardo, The 19*
    *Raphael and La Fornarina 80*
Inquisition, Spanish 42
intonaco 52
Isabella of Castile, Queen of Spain 42
Istanbul *105*

## J

Jonson, Ben *137*
Julian calendar *138*
Julius II, Pope 38, 46-7, 49, 64, 67, 68-9, 78, *79*, 94, 98, 99, 101-102, 104-108
Jupiter, loves of *117*

## K

Knox, John *137*

## L

landscape painting 33
*Laocoön, The 46,* 47, *103*
*Last Judgement, The* (Michelangelo) 48, 51, *60-61*

detail 62, 63
*Last Supper, The* (Leonardo) 16, 18,
  24-5, 32, 34-5
  detail 34, 35
  restoration of 34
Laurentian Library (Florence) 51, 52,
  73-4
Leo IV, Pope 99, *99*
Leo X, Pope 19, 69, 79, *80*, 81, 99,
  102-103, 109
**Leonardo da Vinci**
  anatomical studies 16, *17*, 19, 30,
    31
  drapery studies *30*
  drawings 9, *16-17*, 30, 31, *32*,
    34-5, *35*
  as engineer 15, 16, *16*, 17, 18
  and Guild of St Luke 12, *21*
  handwriting 13, 16
  key dates 12
  Leonardo museums *12, 19*
  life 9, 11-19, 36, 39, 41, 79
  in Milan 15-16, 17, 18, 36
  notebooks 36
  patronage 14
  sexuality 14-15, 16, 19
  *sfumato* 29
  trademarks 33
  *Treatise on Painting* 16, 19, 33
  and Verrocchio 12-13, *150*
  working methods 30-35, 52, 83
  works by:
  *Adoration of the Kings* 9
  *Adoration of the Magi, The* 14
    study for *32*
  *Annunciation, The* 20-21
  *Arno Landscape* 9, *13*
  *Baptism of Christ, The* (detail) *13*
  *Battle of Anghiari* (copy) 18, 30, 32,
    77
  drawings *16-17*, 30, 31, 32, 34, 35,
    77
  *Ginevra de' Benci* 9, *22*
  *Horse and Rider* (bronze) *30*
  *Lady with an Ermine* 23
  *Last Supper, The* 9, 16, 18, 24-5, 32,
    34-5
  *Mona Lisa* 9, 18, 28
  *Old Man and a Youth, An* 15
  *Portrait of a Musician* 31
  *St Jerome* 31
  *St John the Baptist between a Pharisee
    and a Levite* 32-3
  *Self-portrait 8, 11,* (1513) *19*
  *Sforza Monument, The* 15-16, 18
  *Virgin and Child with St Anne, The*
    *29*
  *Virgin and Child with St Anne and
    John the Baptist, The* 26
  *Virgin of the Rocks, The* (c.1483) *9,
    32,* (c.1508) 9, 15, *27*
Lima (Peru) 72
Louis XII, King of France 16, 19, 36,
  104-105, *104*
Luther, Martin 73, 74

**M**

Machiavelli, Niccolo 38-9, *39*, 74
  *The Prince* 38
Machuca, Pedro 72
Maderno, Carlo 70-71
malaria 38
Mantegna, Andrea
  *Agony in the Garden, The* 33, 140

*Dead Christ, The* 140
*Lodovico Gonzaga and his family* 140
marble quarrying 45
Marburg, Protestant University at
  74
Mary, Queen of Scots *137*
Masaccio 51, 52, 66
  *Tribute Money, The* (detail) *52*
Master of Revels 16
Maximilian I, Emperor 105-106, 132
Medici, Alessandro de' 48
Medici, Catherine de' 136-8
Medici Chapel (Florence) 48, *51*, 52,
  73
Medici, Cosimo de' 40
Medici, Lorenzo de' 13-14, 19,
  40-41, 44, 45, 51
  *Tomb of* 48, *51*
Medici, Piero di Lorenzo de' 181
Melzi, Francesco *18*, 19
**Michelangelo Buonarotti**
  architecture 49, 53, 70-71
  and classical art 46, 51, 52
  and Ghirlandaio 44, 52
  and Julius II 46-7, 49, 64, 67
  key dates 45
  life 43-9, 73-4, 79, 81, 101, 115-16
  and the Medicis 44-45, 46, 48
  sexuality 48
  trademarks 53
  working methods 50-53, 64-7,
    115-16
  works by:
  *Awakening Slave, The 51*
  *Bacchus* 9, 46
  *Battle of Cascina, The* 18
    study for 50
  *Battle of the Centaurs, The* 45
  *Capitol, design for the* 49
  *David* 9, 46, 52, *55*, 77
  *Dondi Tondo, The* 50
  *Duomo Pietà* 49
  *Dying Slave, The* 53
  *Fate of Tityus, The* 48
  *Last Judgement, The* 48, 51, *60-61*
    details *62, 63*
  *Laurentian Library* 51, 52, 73-4
  *Medici Tombs* 48, *51*, 52
  *Pietà* 9, 46, *54*
  *Sistine Ceiling, The* 9, 47, 48, *50-51*,
    52, *56-9*, *64-7*, 97
  *Taddei Tondo* 52
  *Tomb of Julius II* 46, *47*, 51
  Milan *15-16*, 17, 18, 36
  *Mona Lisa* (Leonardo) 18, *28*
  Mählberg, Battle of 135

**N**

Naples, Kingdom of 37
Navagero, Andrea 112
Navarre, Jean de 39
Nero, House of (Rome) *102*
Netherlands 136-8
Nicholas V, Pope 68, 100-101, *100*

**O**

oil-painting 31-2, 108-109
Orsini family 36
Ottoman Empire 134
Ovid (Publius Ovidius Naso) *125*, 130

*Metamorphoses* 117, *130*

**P**

Palatine Hill (Rome) 101
Palma Giovane 114, 117
Pantheon (Rome) 81, 100-101, *102*
Paracelsus, Philippus Aureolus 73
Paul III, Pope 48, 49, 61, 69-70, 71,
  *111*
Paul IV, Pope 70, 71
Paul V, Pope 70, 71
Penni, Gianfrancesco 81
Peru 72
Perugino, Pietro 14, 76-7, 78, 83, 86
  *Donation of the Keys, The 77*, 83
  frescoes (Sistine Chapel) 141
  and Leonardo da Vinci 141
  *Pietà, The* 141
  *St Sebastian* 141
Peruzzi, Baldassare 69, 79
Philip II, King of Spain 112, 113,
  114, *130*, 135, *135*
*Pietà* (Michelangelo, St Peter's) 46,
  *54*
*Pietà* (Michelangelo, St Peter's) 46,
Pieve di Ladore (Italy) 108
Pinturicchio, Bernardino
  *Disputation of St Catherine, The* 36
  *Portrait of Alexander VI* 37
Pius III, Pope 38
Pius V, Pope *138*
Pizzaro, Francisco 72
plague 113
Pliny the Elder 51
Porta, Gacomo della 70, 71
printing 8, 42
Protestantism 106, *106*, 134-5
Ponte Vecchio (Florence) 13

**Q**

Quirinal monument, Rome 101, 103

**R**

Raimondi, Marcantonio 79, *113*
  *Judgement of Paris, The* 78
**Raphael Sanzio**
  and Ancient Rome 82, 100-103
  architecture 79-80, 81
  influence of Leonardo on 76, 83,
    84, 88
  and Julius II 78, 79, 80, 98, 101
  key dates 76
  and La Fornarina 80-81
  life 14, 69, 76-81, 100-103, 104
  influence of Michelangelo on 84
  and Perugino 76-7, 78, 83, 86
  trademarks 84
  working methods 82-5, 96-9
  works by:
  *Betrothal of the Virgin, The* 86
  *Deposition* 10
  *Disputà* 84, 98
  *Ecstasy of St Cecilia, The* 83
  *Entombment, The* 89
  *Fire in the Borgo, The* 99
  *Horses of Monte Cavallo, The* 103
  *Judgement of Paris, The* (engraving

  by Raimondi) 78
  *Maddalena Doni* 10
  *Madonna del Granduca* (c.1506) 10,
    84
    detail 85
  *Madonna della Sedia* (Madonna of
    the Chair) 80, *82*
  *Madonna of the Goldfinch, The* 84,
    *88*
  *Mass of Bolsena, The* 99
  *Parnassus, The* 98
  *Portrait of Agnolo Doni* 87
  *Portrait of Castiglione* 78
  *Portrait of Julius II* 79
  *Portrait of Leo X and Two Cardinals*
    *80*
  *St Michael and the Dragon* 82
  *School of Athens* 10, 79, 84, *90-91*,
    96-7, 98
  *Self-portrait 8*, 75, 76
  *Sistine Madonna, The* 10, 94
  *Stanza d'Eliodoro* 79, *92-3*, 99
  *Stanza dell'Incendio* 80, 81, 99
  *Stanza della Segnatura* 79, 84,
    *90-91*, 96-7, 98
  tapestry cartoons 81, 83
  *Transfiguration* 81, 83, 85, 95
  *Triumph of Galatea 8*, 79
Reformation, the 68, 73, 74, 106,
  134-5, *137*
relief sculpture 51-2
Rembrandt van Rijn
  *Stormy Landscape* 33
restoration 34, 67
Romagna, the 38
Romano, Giulio 81
Rome 36-37, *37*, 46-7, *46-7*, 48, 64,
  68-71, 72-4, *73*, 79, 81, *81*, *100-101*,
  100-103, *103*
Rossellino, Antonio
  *Laughing Madonna and Child* 85
Rubens, Peter Paul
  copy of Leonardo's *Battle of
    Anghiari* 18
  *Portrait of Paracelsus* 73
Rustici, Giovanni Francesco 32-3

**S**

Sack of Rome (1527) 47, 48, 69, 72-4,
  112-113, 135
*Sacred and Profane Love* (Titian) 110,
  118-19, 122-3
St Bartholomew's Day Massacre
  136-7, 138
St Peter's Basilica, Rome 37, 41, 47,
  49, 53, 68-71, 80, 81, 102
  consecration of 71
Salai, Giacomo 15, 16, 18, 19
Sangallo, Giuliano da 69
San Lorenzo (Florence) 48, 49, 50
Sansovino, Jacopo 113
Santa Maria dei Fran (Venice) *109*,
  110, 113
Santa Maria delle Grazie (Milan) *41*
Santo Spirito 45
Sanzio, Raphael *see* Raphael Sanzio
Savonarola, Girolamo 9, 40-41, 45-6
*School of Athens, The* (Raphael) 78,
  84, *90-91*, 96-7
sculptural form 52
sculpture 52-3
Scuola di Sant' Antonio (Padua) *109*
'Sea Beggars' (in Dutch
  independence war) 136-7, *138*

Sebastiano del Piombo
  *Portrait of Vittoria Colonna 49*
Seisinegger, Jacob 134
Sforza, Ludovico, Duke of Milan *14,*
  *15-16, 17,* 18, 23, 41
Sforza, Giovanni 37
sfumato 9, 29, 52
silverpoint 31, 32, 97
Sistine Chapel, Rome 47, *48, 50-51,*
  *56-9, 60-63, 64-6, 77,* 81, 85, 87
Sistine Ceiling 47, *50-51, 56-9, 64-5,*
  *66-7,* 85
  restoration of *67*
Sixtus IV, Pope 64
Smyth, William, Bishop of Lincoln
  104
  and Brasenose College, Oxford
  *104*
Sodoma, Il (Giovanni Antonio
  Bazzi) 78
Spain 132-8
Stanza della Segnatura, Rome 78,
  *79, 83, 90-91, 96-7, 98*
Suleiman the Magnificent *73*

# T

tempera 52
*Tempest, The* (Giorgione) *110*
Tintoretto, Jacopo 113, 117, 141
  *Discovery of the Body of St Mark,*
    *The 141*
  *Liberation of Arsinol, The 141*
  and Mannerism 141

*St Mark Freeing a Christian Slave*
  141
Scuola de San Rocco, decoration
  of 141
*Transport of the Body of St Mark 141*
**Titian Vecellio**
  and Alfonso d'Este 109, 110-11,
    114, 125
  and Bellini 108-9, 110, 114
  and Charles V 110, 111, 112, 129,
    132, 133, 134, 135
  financial status 112, *112*
  in Germany 111
  and Giorgione 109, 110, 116
  key dates 108
  life 108-13, 134, 135
  patrons 110-11, 121
  and Philip II 111-12, 113, 114, 130,
    135
  'poesie' 130-31
  tondo 50, 82
  trademarks 116
  working methods 114-17
  workshop 116-17
  works by:
  *Andrians, The* 111, *114-15*
  *Assumption of the Virgin, The* 109,
    110, 116, *124*
  *Bacchus and Ariadne* 111, *125*
  *Battle of Spoleto, The 114*
  *Charles V on Horseback 10,* 129,
    135
  *Christ crowned with Thorns 10*
  *Danäe 130*
  *Death of St Peter Martyr* (copy) *111,*
    116
  *Entombment, The 115*

*Jealous Husband, The 109*
*Man with a Blue Sleeve, The 121*
*Noli Me Tangere 120*
*Pesaro Madonna, The 10*
*Pietà 113,* 116
*Portrait of Aretino 113*
*Portrait of Charles V 132-3*
*Portrait of the Empress Isabella 133*
*Portrait of Federico Gonzaga 110*
*Portrait of Paul III and his Grandsons*
  *111*
*Portrait of Philip II in Armour 114,*
  *135*
*Portrait of Ranuccio Farnese 114*
*Rape of Europa, The 131*
*Sacred and Profane Love* 110, *118-19,*
  *122-3*
*St Mary Magdalen 115,* 116
*Salome 112*
  self-portrait *9, 107*
*Tarquin and Lucretia 116*
  detail *117*
*Venus of Urbino 126-7*
*Young Englishman, The 128*
Torso Belvedere 51, *67*
Toscanelli, Paolo 13
Torrigiano, Pietro 45
Trajan's Column, Rome 101, *103*
Tunis (North Africa) 133, 134

# U

Urban VIII, Pope 71, *71*
Urbino (Italy) 76-7, *76, 78*

# V

Valentino, II (Cesare Borgia), 18,
  36-9, 41, 104
Vasari, Giorgio 12, 13, 30, 32-3, 45,
  50, 51, 64-5, 67, 80, 81, 82, 85, 87,
  108, 111, 114-15
Vatican Palace (Rome) 47, 48, *56-67,*
  73, *78-81, 83-4, 90-93, 96-9,* 102
Vecellio, Titian *see* Titian Vecellio
Venice 104-106, *108-109,* 118-19
*Venus of Urbino* (Titian) *126-7*
Veronese, Paolo 113
  *Rape of Europa, The 117*
Verrocchio, Andrea del 12-13, *14*
  *Baptism of Christ 13*
  *Bust of Lorenzo de' Medici 44, 45*
  *Colleoni Monument, The 14*
  *David* (detail) *14*
Vinci (Tuscany) *12-13*

# W

William, the Silent, Prince of Orange
  136-7, *136*
Wolsey, Cardinal Thomas 74
workshops 12

# Z

Zuccati, Sebastiano 108

WITHDRAWAL